Doing Business in China:
Report from a Field Study Trip

Doing Business in China:
Report from a Field Study Trip

Edited by
Jan Stentoft Arlbjørn
Ole Stegmann Mikkelsen

University Press of Southern Denmark

2013

© The authors and University Press of Southern Denmark
Printed by Grafisk Produktion Odense ApS

ISBN: 978 87 91070 87 7

University Press of Southern Denmark
Campusvej 55
5230 Odense M
Denmark
www.universitypress.dk

Table of Content

Preface..13

Introduction...13
    Organizing the trip...15
    Travel plan..15
    The thank you...16

Chapter 1: Prologue: Why Study Business in China?..........19

Abstract..19
Introduction...19
Population...21
Geography..21
History...22
Politics..22
Religion...23
Education...23
Economy..23
Chinese business in brief...24
Energy..25
Chinese culture in brief..26

Chapter 2: Chinese Business Culture..........................29

Abstract..29
Introduction...29
Research questions..30
Methodology..30
    Empirical studies..31
    Literature review..32
Hofstede's five dimensions..33

- Power distance (PDI) 33
- Individualism (IDV) 34
- Masculinity/Femininity (MAS) 35
- Uncertainty avoidance (UAI) 35
- Long term orientation (LTO) 36

The history of China 37
- Religious belief 37
- The historical development of China 38
  - The beginning of the communist regime 38
  - The transformation of Chinas economy 39
  - Political challenges in China 40

The characteristics of Chinese business culture 42
- Guoqing 42
- Guanxi 43
- Trust and harmony 44
- Face 44

Future China 45
- Doing R&D in China 45
- Chinese management 46
- E-commerce 47
- China becomes individualized 48

Recommendations 48
- Government and five-year plan 48
- Clear strategy 49
- Control mechanism 49
- How to build *guanxi* 49

Reflection 50

Conclusion 51

Chapter 3: Offshoring to China, drivers and barriers...........................52

Abstract 55

Introduction.. 55

Methodology... 57

    Literature review.. 57

    Collection of data 58

    Case study 58

        Company description.. 59

Theoretical reflections 61

    Definitions 61

        Outsourcing 61

        Offshoring.. 61

    Strategic formation 61

        The complexity of a problem - Tame and Wicked problems 62

        The paradox of Deliberateness and Emergentness 62

    Challenges for offshoring in the literature... 63

        Loss of control 64

        Loss of critical skills.. 64

        Loss of flexibility 65

        Hidden cost.. 65

        Culture 65

        Tacit knowledge... 66

        Inventory/transportation cost... 66

        Communication barriers 67

Empirical findings... 67

    Challenges of offshoring in the empirical findings..................................... 67

    Challenge: Loss of critical skills... 68

        Tacit knowledge... 68

- Tacit knowledge: Solutions ... 69
- Quality ... 69
- Quality: Solutions ... 70
- Challenge: Flexibility ... 70
  - Lead-time ... 70
  - Lead-time: Solutions ... 71
  - Costs, stock ... 71
  - Costs, stock: Solutions ... 71
  - R&D ... 72
  - R&D: Solutions ... 72
- Challenge: Hidden costs ... 72
  - Political ... 72
  - Political: Solutions ... 73
  - Economic ... 74
  - Economic: Solutions ... 74
  - Socio cultural ... 74
  - Socio cultural: Solutions ... 75
  - Technological ... 75
  - Technological: Solutions ... 75
- Challenge: Culture ... 76
  - Communication ... 76
  - Communication: Solutions ... 76
  - One child policy ... 76
  - One child policy: Solutions ... 77
  - Face ... 77
  - Face: Solutions ... 77
  - Trust ... 77
  - Trust: Solutions ... 78

- Suppliers 78
- Suppliers: Solutions 78
- Copycats 78
- Copycats: Solutions 79
- Guanxi 79
- Guanxi: Solutions 79
- Challenge: Strategy 79
  - Deliberate - Emergent 79
  - Local – Global 80
- Further findings 80
- Conclusion 82

Chapter 4: Innovation in China 85

- Abstract 85
- Introduction 85
  - Research questions 86
- Methodology 86
- Literature review 87
  - Definitions of the concept of innovation 87
  - Perception of Chinese market 88
  - Chinese understanding of innovation 90
  - Technological trajectories and dynamic capabilities 94
    - Technological trajectories 94
    - Dynamic capabilities 95
  - Definition of the 4P model 96
- Analysis 98
  - Perception of Chinese market 98
  - Integration of cost innovation in business models 100
    - The importance of cost innovation 101

    How does cost innovation influence global competition 102
    Innovative strategies in China 103
    Challenges faced when innovating in China... 106
    How are the case companies innovating in China?................................ 107
    From made in China to made by China.. 110
Conclusion 112
    Further research.. 113

Chapter 5: Corporate Social Responsibility 115

Abstract 115
Introduction... 115
Methodology... 117
Literature review 117
    Approaches to CSR... 117
    Drivers and barriers for CSR 121
        Drivers for companies working with CSR 122
        Barriers for companies working with CSR.. 124
    Auditing and standards 126
        Auditing 126
        Frameworks... 127
Critical aspects of CSR 130
The case study – results from China.. 131
    The approach to CSR in China 131
    Auditing and standards 132
    Drivers and barriers for the Danish companies in China 134
        Drivers in China... 134
        Barriers in China.. 135
The future of CSR in China 139
Where to seek help?.. 139

Conclusion 140
Chapter 6: Epilogue: Learning af Relections **143**
Abstract 143
Introduction.. 143
Most impressive experiences... 144
Application of relevant theories and methods 145
Improved competencies through group work.. 146
Better understanding of Chinese culture.. 147
The most important points of cultural learning 148
Conclusion 149
    Chinese business culture.. 149
    Offshoring to China, drivers and barriers..150
    Innovation in China 151
    Corporate Social Responsibility.. 152
References **155**
Index **165**
About the Editors………………………………………………..**167**

PREFACE

Introduction

This book, entitled "Doing Business in China: Report from a Field Study Trip", contains the students' answers to assignments related to a study trip to China in the period of 6 to 14 October 2012. The study trip was part of the optional subject "International field studies" at Master of Science (M.Sc.) in Business Administration, at the Department of Entrepreneurship and Relationship Management, University of Southern Denmark, Kolding.

The purpose of the field study is, in general, to develop the students' skills to apply specific theories and analysis tools to a general philosophy of science and methodological perspective in actual business problem areas. Furthermore, the purpose is that the students acquire experience with the requirements of international field studies regarding technical as well as social competencies. The aim of the course is to train the students to conduct all phases and facets within a smaller field study including the preparatory desk research part, organization of the fieldwork, and later follow-up analysis and reports.

In the present context, this field study aims to achieve a general knowledge as to doing business and to outline challenges from a Western perspective that should be taken into account, when trading with China. China is an interesting country to study for at least three reasons: 1) The country is undergoing a rapidly economic growth, 2) China is a prioritized destination for outsourcing of production due to wage advantages (Arlbjørn et al., 2013) and 3) The high economic growth makes China attractive from a market perspective (and thus a driver for offshoring). The students have examined fields of study within four topic areas:

- Chinese Business Culture
- Offshoring to China, drivers and barriers
- Innovation in China
- Corporate Social Responsibility (CSR)

The first topic, "Chinese Business Culture" has been chosen because an understanding of cultural differences is perceived as being the overriding success criteria for doing business in China. The second topic is concerned with drivers and barriers for offshoring and outsourcing to China and is selected due to the increasing practice of moving production to China. The third theme is dedicated to innovation. For a long time, China has been known for copying existing products. The theme of innovation has been included to focus on Chinese innovation capabilities in order to provide a deeper understanding of how the Chinese perceive and operate with the concept of innovation. The last chapter is concerned with the important concept of Corporate Social Responsibility that, in a period of truly globalization processes of businesses, becomes even more important to address.

The students have discussed theory and collected data related to the above four topics. In order to be able to report the findings to the companies, it was necessary to write the assignments in English. Furthermore, to increase the ambition level of the assignments, we decided to contact University Press of Southern Denmark for an agreement to publish the assignments. The students responsible for the four book chapters are listed in Table 0.

Chinese Business Culture	Offshoring to China, drivers and barriers	Innovation in China	Corporate Social Responsibility
Mads Davidsen Anja Brink Aaskov Vanesa Breko Sarah Dressel Brian Thorvaldsen	Anna-Sophia Lauritzen Janni Grouleff Nielsen Sisse Levi Hansen Kim Mandrup Hansen Martin Haugegaard	Louise Refsing Rasmussen Anders Ullerup-Aagaard Teis Hørlyck Bech Rasmus Pagh Jensen Anders Norlyk Iversen Anne Fromm-Christiansen	Katrine Illum Nielsen Maria Christensen Jacob Wildt-Andersen Brian Gylling Madsen Birgitte Weinrich Tine Husted Hansen

Table 0: Students divided into the four themes

The students are studying M.Sc. in Management and Leadership and M.Sc. in International Business Development. The M.Sc. line in Management and

Leadership is structured around two central competence areas. The managing part provides knowledge and tools for solving problems regarding SCM, operations management and management accounting. The focus is on the roles and functions in global supply chains and the basic operation systems and philosophies (Just-In-Time, Lean, Agility, etc.). The leadership part ensures understanding of and competence in solving problems within leadership, organizational changes and strategy development.

The M.Sc. line in International Business Development sets focus on the interaction between organizations, be it private companies or public organizations. Specifically, information on international business and market development is communicated as well as insight into theories concerning companies' international business development, marketing and organization. Insight is gained into factors that influence the organizational change processes of the companies and the management of these processes. Whether the area is purchase or sale of products or projects to be carried through in public environment, a number of different employees will be involved in the interaction between two or more organizations. The understanding of the interaction between individuals with different professional and cultural background is considered the key to successful company management.

Organizing the trip

First of all it should be mentioned that the students planned this study trip themselves. There has been a planning period of about 8 months with identifying, contacting and setting up appointments with companies, fundraising, providing communication about the study trip, organizing flights and hotels, transportation to and from companies and sightseeing. In order to solve these tasks, the students organized into different working groups with a representative in a steering group.

Travel plan

The field study trip in 2012 included visits in Shanghai and Beijing. The field study trip began 8th October with a visit at The Royal Danish Consulate General at Shanghai International Trade Center in Shanghai where all groups of students participated. In the afternoon, all four groups visited Nilfisk in Shanghai. In the morning of day two, the four groups were divided into two company visits. Two groups visited Grundfos to uncover outsourcing and CSR issues, and the other two groups visited Alfa Laval to discuss culture and innovation. In the afternoon of day two, the spilt of the entire groups in two sub-groups continued with one visiting DISA and the other with a continued visit at Alfa Laval. Day three was a traveling day with fast train from Shanghai to Beijing. In Beijing the entire groups visited Danfoss in the morning and Novo Nordisk in the afternoon. Friday was a busy day with four visits. The culture and CSR groups visited Morning Tears in the morning, while the innovation and the outsourcing groups visited FLSmidth. In the afternoon, the innovation group visited Beijing International Studies University while the rest of the students visited Coloplast.

The thank you

Many persons have contributed to making this study trip possible. We will therefore thank these people and organizations for their support (time, knowledge and financial support). The persons and organizations are mentioned below.

Funding
Mads Clausens Fond
Ole Kirks Fond
The business economy staff-student committee, University of Southern Denmark, Kolding

Companies that have been visited

Executive Director, Barbara Scheel Agersnap, Danish innovation center Shanghai
Innovation Officer, ICT, Rasmus Duong-Grunnet, Danish innovation center Shanghai
General Manager Greater China, Jens C. Skovrup, Nilfisk
Factory Manager, Lars Kruse Andersen, Alfa Laval
Product Development Manager, Product Centre Asia, Søren Borg, Alfa Laval
President, Eric Bruner, DISA
Grundfos
Gloria /Li Jinhuan, Danfoss

Senior Manager, Finance and Business Strategy, Jakob Posselt Novo Nordisk (China)
Ange Moray, Morning Tears
CEO Anders Bech, FLSchmidt Beijing Ltd.
Professor Zhang Xihua, Beijing International Studies University BISU
CEO Vagn Heiberg, Coloplast Beijing

People with inspiration and technical support
Henrik Olsson, Howe A/S

This book would not have been possible without the financial support of four companies/organizations. Therefore we thank Tresu Production Systems A/S, Toosbuys Fond, Bredana Data System and Viking Safe-Life Equipment for financial support.

Finally, we would like to thank the students for a well-organized field study trip and for their proactive learning attitude. Beyond excelling in company visits with discussions and factory tours, they contributed with events to make this trip also a fun experience. We certainly believe that this trip has given the students a learning experience - technically, socially and culturally.

Best regards and hopefully enjoyable reading.

Kolding, October 2013

Jan Stentoft Arlbjørn	Ole Stegmann Mikkelsen
Professor, Ph.D.	Post.doc., Ph.D.

CHAPTER 1

Prologue: Why study Business in China?

Jan Stentoft Arlbjørn and Ole Stegmann Mikkelsen

Abstract

This chapter aims to explain why one should consider doing business in China. The chapter contains facts about China, information about the population, geography, history, politics, religion, education, economy, energy and culture in order to illustrate that there are many business opportunities in China.

Introduction

The following section is based on information from the World Bank.[1] China, officially called The People's Republic of China, is located in East Asia. China is one of the world's most populated countries with more than 1.3 billion people, which equals approx. 20 percent of the earth's population. China is the second largest economy in the world measured by nominal GDP and the largest importer and exporter of goods. The country is known for having the world's second largest military budget, with the largest mobile army.

Today, China is one of the few countries that officially profess to the communistic ideology and China's Communist Party still controls monopolistically. Since the first reforms in 1979 China has moved from plan economy towards market based economy and experienced a fast economic and social development. Growth rates of GDP at 10 percent per

---

[1] http://www.worldbank.org/en/country/china/overview - accessed 3/10-2013

year have moved more than 500 million people out of poverty. Ranked as number 90 in the world, China's GDP per capita in 2012 was 6,188 $.

China's 12th five year plan (2011-2015) is focusing on development and growth in order to solve environmental and social differences. The aim is to reduce pollution in order to increase the energy effectiveness, to improve access to education and healthcare. China is a member of economy organizations such as UN, G-20, WTO, APEC, BRICS and BCIM.

Population	1,350,695,000 (2012)
Capital	Beijing
Largest town	Shanghai
Area	9,600,000 km2 (3,705,405 square miles)
Form of government	One party state (Communist party)
Head of state	President Xi Jinping, Vice President Li Yuanchao
Head of government	Li Keqiang
Language	Mandarin, Yue (Cantonese), Wu (Shanghainese), Minbei (Fuzhou), Minnan (Hokkien-Taiwanese), Xiang, Gan, and Hakka dialects, as well as minority languages.
Inhabitants	Han 92 %, others (Zhuang, Manchu, Uygur, Hui, Yi, Miao, Tibetan, Mongol, Korean etc.) 8 %
Religion	Taoist, Buddhist, Muslim
Currency	Yuan (also called Renminbi)
Average lifespan	Men 72 years; women 75 years (2011)
GDP per Capita (2012):	U.S. $ 6,188 (2012)
GDP	U.S. $ 8,358,363,135 (2012)
GDP (real growth)	7,8 % (2012)
One child policy	Introduced in 1978 in order to limit the growth of the population.

Table 1.1: Facts about China[2]

---

[2] http://databank.worldbank.org/data/views/reports/tableview.aspx?isshared=true&ispopular=country&pid=1 & http://english.gov.cn/links/brief20050923.htm, accessed 7/19-2013;

Population[3]

With the world's largest population China also has the world's largest labour force and the largest potential market for goods and services.

The size of the population also causes various problems, e.g. inadequate food supply, lack of employment and low incomes. China has carried through census five times in; 1953, 1964, 1982, 1990 and 2000. In addition local population registers are carried out each year and accumulated at a national level. Census and registers indicate high growth rates in population during the 1950s and from 1964 to 1973, but with a moderate growth since 1973. In order to reduce the growth rate the Chinese government launched family planning campaigns four times; 1956-58, 1962-66, 1971-79 and the current one child campaign from 1979. The goal was to reduce the number of children per family to one before 1985 and then to maintain this until year 2000. As a consequence the gender distribution now shows an overweight of males.

Geography

China covers a total area of 9.6 million square kilometres on the world map and crosses four time zones, but has one official central time. China has a border line of 22.800 kilometer and shares borders with fourteen countries: Vietnam, Laos, Burma, India, Bhutan, Nepal, Pakistan, Afghanistan, Tajikistan, Kyrgyzstan, Kazakhstan, Russia, Mongolia and North Korea. China shares sea borders with South Korea, Japan, Vietnam and the Philippines. This massive geographic area includes different geological structures and thereby varying forms of landscape. This changing geography causes a diverse climate from tropical in the South to subarctic in North East China. The geography also causes an uneven distribution of the population, as 94 percent live in 1/3 of the Eastern parts of the country. The areas near the coast are more economically developed and therefore China experiences a high number of migrants from the rural regions to the coastal areas. The Shandong province with the mild coast climate has more

---

[3]http://www.denstoredanske.dk/Samfund%2c_jura_og_politik/%c3%98konomi/%c3%98konomi_i_andre_lande/Kina_(%c3%98konomi, accessed d. 17/9-2013

than 90 million citizens while Tibet with its mountain climate has no more than 3 million citizens.[4]

History[5]

The history of China can be described through its different dynasties, with the first being the Xia Dynasty dating back to 2070-1600 BC, followed by the Shang and Zhou Dynasty. The Qin Dynasty lasted from 221 – 206 BC - in this period many lasting changes were made such as a standardization of the language, measures and currency. The Qin Dynasty was followed by the Han Dynasty from 206 BC to 220 AD, which marked the beginning of military power. With the collapse of the Han Dynasty, China was divided into three kingdoms. In 580 AD China was reunited under the Sui Dynasty followed by a series of dynasties. The last imperial dynasty in China – the Qing Dynasty – lasted until 1912.

During the first half of the twentieth century China experienced the fall of the Chinese emperor, the Japanese invasion, World War II and a civil war. On January 1st 1912 the People's Republic of China was established with general Yuan Shikai as president. After his dead the country was divided into regional governments, the political division continued and in 1927 resulted in the Chinese civil war between the nationalistic Kuomintang (KMT) and the communist party (CPC). The war divided China into: China in Taiwan and China. On October 1st, 1949, The People's Republic of China was proclaimed by Mao Zedong. China "regained" Hong Kong from Great Britain in 1997 and Macao from Portugal in 1999.

Politics[6]

The Communist Party of China was founded in Shanghai in 1921 by 12 people, among others Mao Zedong. At the top of the party is the Central Committee. The party is a unified entity organized according to its constitution and the principle of democratic centralism. The political structure of China is quite complex. In short, the People's Congress System

---

[4] http://travel.nationalgeographic.com/travel/countries/china-facts/ & http://www.mapsofworld.com/china/, accesses 3/10 - 2013
[5] http://english.gov.cn/2005-08/06/content_24233.htm, accessed 3/10-2013
[6] http://english.mofcom.gov.cn/aarticle/zm/201205/20120508132541.html & http://www.china.org.cn/english/features/state_structure/64404.htm, accessed 3/10 - 2013

is China's central political system and consists of National People's Congress and People's Congresses, at which the members are directly elected. The main functions of the National People's Congress are legislating and revising laws, approving the government budget and electing and removing officials. The highest organ of state power is The National People's Congress, which holds the power to elect and remove the leaders of the Supreme People's Court and the Supreme People's Procuratorate. The National People's Congress consists of representatives elected by the provinces, autonomous regions and municipalities as well as deputies elected by the armed forces. The election period is five years.

Religion[7]

Officially the Chinese government is atheistic, however religious activities are generally permitted. It is difficult to measure the number of followers to the different religions since many Chinese belong to more than one religious tradition. The most widely spread organized religions are Buddhism, Islam, Roman Catholic and Protestant Christianity, Taoism, Shamanism, Orthodox Christianity and Confucianism that has some religious aspects, which are also found as the basis for a large part of the Chinese society.

Education[8]

The educational system in China is governed by the Ministry of Education. The Chinese government promised free teaching to pupils in nine years from elementary school to middle school, and education is therefore mandatory from the age of 6 to the age of 15. In the urban areas most children also have the opportunity to attend high school for three years. Illiteracy in China has fallen from 80 to approx. 5 percent among the young and mid-aged part of the population.

Economy

From the beginning of the 1950s to the late 1970s China was a centrally controlled plan economy. However, since the early 1980s, when Deng Xiaoping came to power, the economy system has gradually been reformed. Today, the economy has the world's highest growth rates on average 10

---

[7] http://english.gov.cn/2006-02/08/content_182603.htm, accessed 3/10-2013
[8] http://english.gov.cn/2006-02/08/content_182560.htm, accessed 3/10-2013

percent since the late 1970s. The economic policy during Deng was dominated by initiatives, which enabled growth in society by opening the economy towards other countries. The reforms began in agriculture and spread to other industries. The economic structure continued to change with lessened contributions to GDP by the main sector and to higher contributions by the secondary and tertiary industries. The growth in China is unevenly distributed among regions, with a more rapid growth in the east coast provinces – in which the main parts of the foreign investments are made and where the export to the world market is highest. [9]

China is currently the world's second largest economy, largest merchandise exporter, second largest merchandise importer, second largest destination of foreign direct investment (FDI) and largest manufacturer. China´s main trading partners in regard to exports are the European Union, United States, Hong Kong, Japan and the Republic of Korea. The global economic crisis that began in 2008 has significantly affected China's economy. The exports, imports, and FDI inflows declined, and GDP growth slowed. The Chinese government reacted by implementing a $586 billion economic package to provide incentives for increasing domestic consumption. Among other things these policies contributed to China weathering the effects of the global fall in demand. While several of the world's leading economies experienced negative or stagnant economic growth, China's real GDP growth averaged 9.6 percent from 2008 to 2011.[10]

Chinese business in brief

In 2004 there were 242.000 foreign financed companies in China with a work force of more than 10 million, which contributed to China's foreign trade with 57 percent. Since the early 1990s large, high-technology and transnational companies have played an increasingly important role in regard to investments. Previously these investments came especially from Hong Kong, Taiwan and Macao, and the companies were small and labour intensive. Deng's economic reforms from 1979 lead to changes through

---

[9]http://www.denstoredanske.dk/Samfund,_jura_og_politik/%C3%98konomi/%C3%98konomi_i_andre_lande/Kina_(%C3%98konomi), accessed 17/9-2013
[10]http://stat.wto.org/CountryProfile/WSDBCountryPFView.aspx?Language=E&Country=CN & http://fpc.state.gov/documents/organization/194783.pdf, accessed 19/9-2013

market economic experiments and opening for foreign investment and technology. In 1979 four special economic free zones were established in Guangdong (Shenzhen and Zhuhai) and Fujian (Xiamen and Shantou) provinces. The purpose of the zones is to attract capital. In 1989 the island Hainan became the fifth economic zone.[11]

The new China (Shanghai) Free Trade Experiment Zone is expected to open officially this year (2013), covering the Waigaoqiao Free Trade Zone, Yangshan port, the Pudong Airport area and the Waigaoqiao Logistics Bonded Zone. It is expected that the new free trade experiment zone in Shanghai will be different, although it is not exactly known in which way.

According to the Ministry of Commerce, China attracted in 2012 $111.72 billion in FDI, which was a decrease of 3,7 percent from the previous year. During the first six months in 2013 foreign investors established 10,630 companies in China, and FDI inflow increased by 4.9 percent to $61.98 billion. The service sector continues to top the manufacturing sector with an increase of approx. 12 percent in the first half of 2013, and the sector had a FDI inflow of $30.63 billion.[12]

Energy

Unfortunately the rapid industrial development increased the level of pollution, and today China has some of the world most polluted cities in respect to air quality.

China is the largest manufacturer and user of coal. China's economy is depending on coal, which counts for 2/3 of the country's energy consumption. China has the world's third largest coal reserves and since 1989 the world's largest coal production. Around 80 percent of the coal reserves are located in North China, leading to a high level of coal transport to East and South China. However, there is a move on-going from coal to water resources like Three Gorges Dam.[13]

In 2011, 9.4 percent of China's energy consumption came from non-fossil fuels. In accordance with the recent five-year plan, increased attention has

---

[11] [http://www.denstoredanske.dk/Samfund, jura og politik/%C3%98konomi/%C3%98konomi i andre lande/Kina (%C3%98konomi)](http://www.denstoredanske.dk/Samfund,_jura_og_politik/%C3%98konomi/%C3%98konomi_i_andre_lande/Kina_(%C3%98konomi)) , accessed 17/9-2013

[12] http://www.chinadaily.com.cn/cndy/2013-07/26/content_16833794.htm, accessed 19/9-2013

[13] [http://www.denstoredanske.dk/Geografi og historie/Kina og Mongoliet/Kina generelt/Kina (Geografi)](http://www.denstoredanske.dk/Geografi_og_historie/Kina_og_Mongoliet/Kina_generelt/Kina_(Geografi)), accessed 19/9-2013

been paid to renewable energy. At the same time China produced more renewable power than any other nation, which was around one-fifth of the world's total. In 2011 China invested USD 52 billion in renewable energy, which placed the country among top-five regarding total investment in renewable power. Although China is a global leader, its growth in renewable energy investments slowed during 2011. At this time China made massive investments to meet its growing energy needs. This caused significant increases in access to grid-connected electricity.[14]

Chinese culture in brief[15]

The Chinese culture may be perceived as complicated since it builds on other values than Western values.

Confucianism: Refers to a set of ethical beliefs authored by the Chinese philosopher Confucius (551-479 BC). The Confucian thought is centred around the idea that a person can achieve moral perfection through constant soul-searching and a strong feeling of duty to family and society. The basic principles can be summed up as a moral codex or an ethic belief.

Guanxi: Means a personal relationship and stands for any type of relationship. Throughout his whole life the individual Chinese creates a network of connections through mutual favours. Social relations between Chinese people are based on a relative status between them. One favour deserves another and is therefore expected to be returned. Guanxi as relationships are developed over time, in many cases without a specific "need" or "use" for the relationship.

Mianxi: is rooted in Confucianism and means face. Face is very important and needs to be considered at all times. In private as well as in business is it important for Chinese people not to lose face. Therefor any action that can result in this should be avoided.

The language: Generally, negative answers are considered disrespectful. A Chinese will only rarely say "no". Instead he will answer ambivalently by saying "perhaps", "I need to think about it", "let us see" - which normally

---

[14] http://www.china.org.cn/business/2012-02/10/content_24601666.htm & http://www.map.ren21.net/GSR/GSR2012_low.pdf, p. 23, 62, 87, accessed 19/9-2013

[15] http://www.ifc.org/wps/wcm/connect/aeae62804b7321708fcdcfbbd578891b/IFC+PSO+26+052112.pdf?MOD=AJPERES & http://www.ediplomat.com/np/cultural_etiquette/ce_cn.htm, accessed 19/9-2013

means "no". Strong emotional expressions should be avoided as they are perceived as a lack of balance and overview.

Form of address: A Chinese will first tell you the surname followed by the first name. Avoid speaking to a person, using only surname first name. Chinese people generally introduce their guests using their full titles and company name, since this is ascribed high value.

Business cards: Exchanging business cards is very important in China. It is through this exchange you will be remembered. When you receive a business card, it should be received with both hands.

CHAPTER 2

Chinese Business Culture

Mads Davidsen, Anja Brink Aaskov, Vanesa Breko, Sarah Dressel and Brian Thorvaldsen

Abstract

This study is based on Chinese business culture and what Danish companies should be aware of when entering China. Throughout the study in China, several Danish and foreign companies contributed with their experiences in/from China. This assignment is based on their experiences, and the purpose of it is to get Danish companies closer to China and create more understanding of the business culture. China's religious beliefs and its historical, economic and political developments are described as important factors of the way of doing business in modern China. Guanxi, trust and the prevention of losing face are still three essential aspects describing Chinese business culture. Chinese and Western business culture differ a lot from each other. In China focus lies in close relations and trust whereas Western companies are more interested in transactions. Furthermore, China's development in the future will have an impact on foreign companies. These impacts are important to face for foreign companies, especially in order to utilize the potential possibilities.

Introduction

For many years, Western companies have seen China as a low-cost country (The Economist, 2012). Today, the Chinese market has become of great interest for Western countries due to new market opportunities. Despite enormous Western interests in China, the country still remains a dream for many Western companies, including Danish companies (Fang, 2006). In fact, a lot of business conflicts seem to be related to cultural issues, as cultural behaviour exists behind every business relationships (Faure et al., 1998, p. 137-148). The lack of a deeper understanding of Chinese business negotiating style, and how to do business with the Chinese, may have contributed to the fact that Western managers are still failing to manage business relations in China (Björkman & Kock, 1995, pp. 519-535). The challenge like "how do we prepare ourselves to do business in China? is crucial of becoming successful. Another challenge is how to prepare managers and employees to deal with the cultural differences (Hansen, 2012a). For some Danish companies it has led to a drawback in terms of investing in China, while other companies are still struggling to become successful in China.

This chapter points out characteristics about Chinese business culture. It is important to understand the way Chinese people do business. It closely examines the foundation of Chinese business behaviour compared to the values which characterize the Danish business style. To provide information about the Chinese behaviour a description of China's development in a historical perspective is needed. Particularly it includes a description of the political system and religious beliefs which can identify core values of the way Chinese do business. The history of China will be combined with empirical studies from China, including interviews with Danish and other Western companies. The combination of China's historical development and empirical studies will bring a better understanding of the Chinese business culture as it might be perceived today.

Research questions

Danish companies are facing a number of challenges when doing business in China. The purpose of this chapter is to answer the following research questions.

1. *What is the foundation of Chinese business culture?*
2. *What is essential for Danish companies to be aware of when entering China?*
3. *How will China develop in the future?*

Methodology

As preparation for the field studies, theoretical research was carried out to create a framework for the empirical analyses. The framework relies on Geert Hofstede's (1991) five dimensions supported by other scientific articles and literature which are relevant to this research in particular. Hofstede defines culture as the *software of the mind* that guides us in our daily interactions (Hofstede, 1991). Hofstede is comprehensive in an approach to understand the overall business values of China compared to Denmark. Hofstede's five dimensions may also give some identification of Chinese business culture and some general patterns of social behaviour and lifestyle. The understanding of the Chinese business culture and the potential development and future trends is useful knowledge for Danish business people who want to do business in China. By using Hofstede's five dimensions it brings a description of the human culture, the cultural differences and the cultural conflicts (Pub, 2012).

As a supplement to Hofstede's dimension, the article "Negotiation: the Chinese style" by Tony Fang (1999) will be included in particular. According to Tony Fang, there are two perspectives in the cultural theory and social behaviour: the etic approach and the emic approach. The etic paradigm is recognized and used by Hofstede, which is the culture in general. The emic approach is the specific approach which acknowledges that culture in the global context is much more complex in contrast to the etic approach (Fang, 2006).

China consists of more than 1.2 billion inhabitants. Due to this fact it might be impossible to describe China from the same set of values, symbols and characteristics (Fang, 2006). Furthermore, the theoretical research will also include other scientific articles and literature supporting the studies.

Empirical studies

The empirical survey was conducted in China with the use of a semi-structured interview guide. The framework for the interviews was primarily made before entering China. However, some questions were modified in China due the interview process and other observations made in China.

Eight interviews were completed in China with representatives from Danish and foreign companies or institutions. The interviews consist of Danish and Western companies with more than ten years of business experience in China. The companies are all geographically located in the regions around Beijing and Shanghai. Furthermore, the interviewed persons were all employees at a management level. Because of the companies' desire to be anonymous, it will not be pointed out which company that said what in this study. Furthermore in relation to the empirical findings, some articles have been included in order to clarify the opinions from the interviews in China.

The empirical approach has created limitations on how to understand Chinese culture. One limitation might be that the main part of the interviewed people has a Western-oriented background. This may affect the way companies are organized in China and how they do business. However, some companies did surprisingly enough include Chinese employees as a part of the interview. The Chinese employees involved in some cases were strategic managers and in other cases operational workers. The purpose was to introduce the cultural differences and similarities between the West and China from both perspectives. The participation was also valuable in terms of how the employees individually perceived the Chinese business culture. This was useful in order to compare the theoretical research of Hofstede and Fang with the empirical research.

Literature review

Geert Hofstede's five dimensions will be used through the study to identify and compare Chinese and Danish culture. The use of Hofstede's theory will provide characteristics and specific understanding of Chinese culture compared to Danish culture. Hofstede's theory is based on Inkele's and Levisions' extensive IBM study in which they examined national cultures. The dimensions are power distance, collectivism/individualism, femininity/masculinity and uncertainty avoidance (Hofstede, 2012a; Hofstede 2012b). Furthermore, Hofstede has in his subsequent research added a fifth dimension in the national culture, long-term/short-term orientation (Confucian Dynamism) according to his research in China (Fang, 2006). Because of the critique of Hofstede and his obsolete dimensions, Hofstede's five cultural dimensions will primarily be used to compare his dimensions with the contents of this assignment. Do his dimensions still have an impact on culture today? In addition to this, *culture theory* by Edward T. Hall and Richard Gesteland will also be utilized in order to obtain a broader understanding of culture as a phenomenon. Edward T. Hall is known for his high and low context culture. When companies are abroad, it is important to pay attention to the patterns in the exact country, which characterize the business partners, in low and high context cultures. This could help understand the international culture, and by the understanding the company properly can get more influence on the cooperation. Gesteland is using many concepts in the cultural theory, which he has collected from a variety of sources and then transferred into simple terms.

Besides Hofstede's theory, an article of Yadong Luo (1997) stresses the essential principles of *guanxi*. Furthermore, Irene Yeung and Rosalie Tung describe *guanxi* and how to gain *guanxi*. This is useful for Danish companies when starting business in China.

Hofstede's five dimensions

Based on Hofstede's IBM study, China and Denmark are assigned a value in each of the five cultural dimensions. These values indicate how the country is characterized on the culture dimension compared with another country. Hofstede's research is comparative which means that the dimensions for each country is relative and the dimensions make only sense compared with other countries. Hofstede defines culture as an average mental mind which distinguishes a group of people. Hofstede's dimensions contribute to a general characteristic of a nation (Fang, 2003). Figure 2.1 illustrates Hofstede's cultural dimension of China and Denmark.

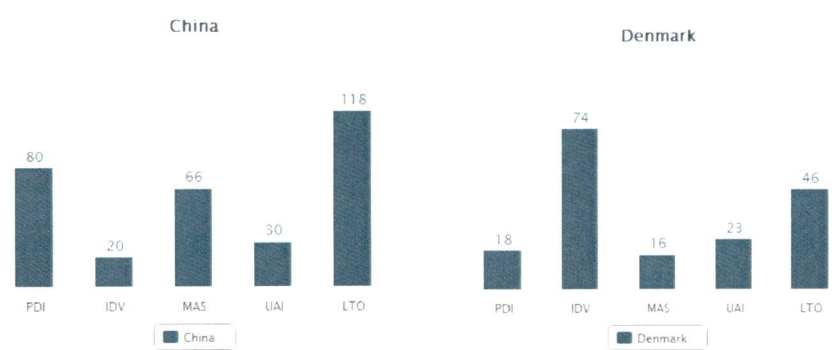

Figure 2.1: Comparing China and Denmark
Source: Own making with inspiration from Hofstede

Power distance (PDI)

Power distance is defined as *"The extent to which the less powerful members of institutions and organizations within a country expect and accept that power is distributed unequally"* (Hofstede, 2012a).

In this index, China scores 80 points, which puts China at the top of the index level (Hofstede, 2012a). This means that the culture accepts inequalities amongst people, both at family level as well at the organizational level (Hofstede, 2012a). According to Fang, the social hierarchy faces individual right. The individual must tribute to the social order to maintain the wanted social stability and harmony (Fang, 1999). In the Danish workplaces, equality, comfort, individuality and democracy are in focus. The workplaces are often characterized like open office environment and the social manner at work is informal. In relation to this, the communications are directly and it is allowed to say your opinion if you disagree. The power is decentralized in the organizations and Danes believe in self-management to a certain degree. Danes are coaching and leading instead of managing. This means that Danes solve problems, plan and organize - identifying deviations from the plan and monitor results instead of direct leadership. Furthermore this is characterized by a determination of direction, in which the leadership develops a vision for the future and achieves strategies for the necessary changes to realize the vision (Hofstede, 2012a).

Individualism (IDV)

Individualism is characterized as *"The degree of interdependence a society maintains among its members"* (Hofstede, 2012a).

China has a score of 20, which means that it is a highly collectivist culture (Hofstede, 2012a). Regarding their workplace this means that they are not necessary committed to the company they work for, but maybe they are committed to their colleagues (Hofstede, 2012a). According to Hofstede, cultures of high power distance have a tendency towards a little individualism. Relations are very important in the Chinese society – both in their business environment as well in their private life. Trust, relationship and groups are very important in a collectivistic Chinese culture (Fang, 2006). Compared to Danes, their business culture applies an easy way of doing business. Danes have a direct form of communication and it is not necessary to build up a relationship before doing business. Denmark scores 74 in individualism. This means that Danes are expected to take care of themselves and prefer loosely-knit framework in their work life. Conversely the Chinese people belong to groups, where they can take care of each other (Hofstede, 2012b).

Comparing the scores between the two countries indicates a different approach in doing business. In relation to Edward T. Hall, his culture theory of China applies to a polychronic culture, because they have a great focus on the contexts – the process and relation instead of explicit statements (Gesteland, 2012).

Masculinity/Femininity (MAS)

"The fundamental issue here is what motivates people, wanting to be the best (masculine) or liking what you do (feminine)" (Hofstede, 2012a).

China is a masculine society with a score of 66. According to Hofstede the culture is success oriented and driven. An example is the Chinese students who are competitive-minded and are aiming to achieve success and high exam scores (Hofstede, 2012a). Denmark scores 16 in the masculine dimension, which means that it is a feminine country. Danes prefer balance between the workplace and spare time. In the business environment, managers strive towards consensus and prioritize values as solidarity, equality and well-established working conditions. Danes are willing to discuss conflicts because they seek to find the right solution (Hofstede, 2012b).

Uncertainty avoidance (UAI)

Uncertainty avoidance is characterized as *"The extent to which the members of a culture feel threatened by ambiguous or unknown situations and have created beliefs and institutions that try to avoid these"* (Hofstede, 2012a).

China has a low score of 30 (Hofstede, 2012a). This score implies that Chinese are entrepreneurial and adaptable. Ambiguity is a part of the Chinese society (Hofstede, 2012a). They also have an urge to work hard and an emotional need for rules. The Chinese people prefer a stable job – then they feel safe and proud. In relation to risk taking, the Chinese would prefer to work in groups rather than independently (Nielsen et al., 2005). Denmark scores only 23 points. The drive is curiosity and creativity. In their work life, it is accepted that things change over a short horizon. Danish combination of individualism and a high degree of curiosity cause good skills in innovation and design (Hofstede, 2012b). Another factor in the Danish work life is that they are not afraid of ambiguous situations.

Long term orientation (LTO)

Long term orientation is described as *"the extent to which a society shows a pragmatic future-oriented perspective rather than a conventional historical short-term point of view"* (Hofstede, 2012a).

China is a highly long-term oriented society with a score of 118. The Chinese are insistent and can adapt to new terms rather quickly (Hofstede, 2012a). The culture believes that time, situations and context depend on trust. Generally they have strong ability to invest and high level of patience to achieve goals (Hofstede, 2012a).

Conversely Denmark has a score of 46. Danes has a short-term orientation society. In the Danish business culture, there is a focus on the present and not the future. Danes prefer analytical thinking and rationality in the business culture (Hofstede, 2012b).

In relation to Hall's theory about low versus high context culture, it differs in a way of communication. The Chinese culture is highly contextual which can result in many unwritten rules, which can be confusing for Danes, who belong to a low contextual culture. Chinese have respect for property, and the human interaction is valued. Danes, on the contrary, need detailed information about their business relations, with whom they are in contact with. For the Danes, the task is more important than the relationship (Changingminds, 2012). Hall argues that the general culture analyses by Hofstede are either monochronic or polychronic. The terms monochron and polychron have to do with our time sense – how the culture manage and perceive time. Polychrons prefer to keep their time in workplace unstructured, then they can move from one activity to another. Polychrons can meet deadlines, but in their own way. They does not prefer detailed and organizing plans, they want to follow their own internal mental processes and thoughts about time. Monochronic time means careful planning and doing one thing at a time. Monochrons love to plan in detail, making lists and organizing their time into daily routine. Denmark is a monochronic culture. Contracts are taken seriously and the key word is efficiency. Danes prioritize their job at first and pay attention to time – in a business environment, China places more emphasis on human capital and social relationships than sticking to plans (Changingminds, 2012).

The history of China

As a part of our research on Chinese business culture, the following section will be divided into two groups; religious beliefs and the historical development of China.

Religious belief

The Chinese culture is built upon three philosophical traditions: Confucianism, Taoism, and Buddhism. The Confucianism philosophy is based upon human relationships; Taoism focuses on life in harmony with nature, while Buddhism deals with people's immortal world (Fung, 1966, p. 12).

The mixture of Confucianism, Taoism, and Buddhism must be perceived as philosophies rather than religions (Fung, 1966, p. 12). China has no official religion as China has been a Communist lead country since 1949. Religious beliefs are monitored by the Bureau of Religious Affairs, which was established in 1954 (Bargfeldt, 2012). The five permitted religions are Confucianism, Buddhism, Taoism, Islam and Christianity (Udenrigsministeriet, 2012). Officially, the majority of the Chinese population declare themselves as atheist or as non-religious (Bargfeldt, 2012).

In some cases, the philosophies may explain why the Chinese people can be considered immensely flexible and adaptable – according to Hofstede's dimension *Uncertainty avoidance.* In order to further our understanding on how these philosophies influence the way Chinese people do business, it is significant to dig further into each philosophy.

Confucianism is a form of moral ethic and a practical philosophy of human relationship and conduct (Tu, 1984). It includes values, which involves moral cultivation, importance of interpersonal relationships, including the concepts of trust, *guanxi* and *guoqing*. Furthermore, it regards family orientation, respect for age and hierarchy, avoidance of conflict and need for harmony and concept of face (Hofstede & Bond, 1988, pp. 5-21).

Buddhism is a religion, which builds upon learning that Buddha preached about after his enlightenment. Buddha's first name was Siddhartha and he discovered that life was combined with poverty, illness and dead. He walks on India's country roads to find the truth about life and salvation. Buddha means the enlightened. The religion have about 250-300 million believers phrased China (Religion, 2012).

Taoism can be described through the principles of Yin-Yang, which is a symbol that in a Western context can be translated into "shadow & light" (Porkert, 1974). Yin represents female elements such as moon, night, water, weakness, darkness, mystery, softness, passivity, etc. Yang represents male elements such as sun, day, fire, strength, brightness, clearness, hardness, activity, etc. (Chen, 2001). Yin and Yang depend on each other, exist within each other, give birth to each other, and succeed each other at different points in time (Fang, 2006).

Some Chinese describe the Chinese culture as closely related to the principal of Feng Shui as well. Feng Shui can be correlated to Taoism. The principal of Feng Shui is to create harmony between humans and their surroundings. Practitioners of Feng Shui believe it has a positive impact on health, wealth and personal relationships (Wydra, 1996, p. 30)

The inspiration of the Buddhism philosophy is to be found in the principles of Yin-Yang as well (Fang, 2006).

Some cultural theorists claim these three philosophies as the overall foundation of Chinese culture, which reflects the way China is doing business (Fang, 2006). In many ways, Confucianism, Taoism and Buddhism give the Chinese people power to absorb things that are good and beneficial. According to the cultural theorists, the Chinese culture has survived due to this certain power (Fang, 2006).

The historical development of China

This section presents some turning points in the historical development of China, which are still visible in Chinese society today. This involves a brief description of Mao Zedong and the beginning of the communist regime followed by Deng Xiaoping and the economic transformation in 1979. Mao and Deng's leadership have had a great impact on the Chinese culture, but also on the political challenges that China is facing today.

The beginning of the communist regime

For more than 60 years, China has been a communist regime. Mao Zedong established the Central Committee of the Communist Party in 1949 with inspiration from the Soviet Union. Mao changed everything that was built upon feudalism and capitalism into Marxist and social ideals. Feudalism is a form of society, where promises about war-favours were exchanged with land in an in advance of determinant hierarchical system. Feudalism has its roots from the Middle-Ages, where for example the common peasant could acquire a piece of land if he yields war-favours for the lord (History, 2012).

Capitalism refers to an economic and social system where rights to property and means of production are private and where capacity for work, advantages and capital are managed in one market. Capitalism builds upon a laissez-faire principal about a free market where the individuals can exchange goods and services without the States intervention. This interpretation can vary from country to country. Capitalism is often mistaken with liberalism, but capitalism is an economic system and liberalism is an ideology.

The Chinese society was structured by a powerful and bureaucratic government. Many Chinese believe the economic, technological and cultural foundations of modern China were laid through Mao's policies. Mao transformed the country from an agrarian society into a major world power (History, 2012).

From 1949 until 1976, China was a closed country. Human upbringing and retraining in terms of erroneous ideas was an important tool in Mao's socialist reforms (Leksikon, 2012). Some interviews in China have pointed out the fact that Chinese people were not allowed to travel outside China during Mao's regime. Nor were the Chinese allowed to decide which education or religious belief they preferred.

Furthermore, Mao's regime carefully controlled the movement from countryside to Chinese cities. Until Mao's death, 80 percent of the population lived in the country side and only 20 percent in urban areas. Since then, over 300 million Chinese have moved to great cities like Shanghai and Beijing (Hansen & Birk, 2012).

The transformation of Chinas economy

A major turning point in the history of China happened in 1978, when Deng Xiaoping gained power. Deng opened China from an economic point of view. The economic reforms created a much greater interaction with Western universities. As one interview states *"The Chinese were not allowed to travel outside China and get free education. Today, they are allowed to travel and get a free education. That was not the case one generation ago"* (Case A). According to some interviews in China, Deng's transformation created curiosity and new possibilities for the Chinese people. *"The openness [...of Chinas economy] creates possibilities, but also stress and competition"* (Case A). Competition suddenly became an issue for the Chinese people, as one company points out. Until

1978 competition was an unknown subject in China. Some of the interviews argue that globalization is the reason for Chinas rapid adaption and learning skills. This change in behaviour was caused by the increasing information that flowed into China. One interview pointed out *"Many Chinese were working for multinational companies and thereby had access to new foreign information"* (Case D). During the 1980's and 1990's, the high economic growth and social welfare were contributed to the West, meaning Europe and America.

Since Deng Xiaoping introduced the one-child policy in 1979, the goal was not only to reduce the population rate, but also to improve the living conditions of the populace. Entry exams for universities were reinstated after they had been abolished under Mao's regime. The goal was to create an elite of highly educated students that could lead China towards becoming a world leader. The education system became a vital social institution (Nie, 2010).

The Chinese have often been perceived as hardworking people. One of the reasons is to be found in the family orientation where a lot of Chinese provide a great social and financial support to one or two elder generations within the family. Chinese people are socialized people who take great responsibility in securing the heritage of family. This explains China's low score on Hofstede's dimension *Individualism.*

According to the empirical studies in China, the economic development has created a greater gap between the rapid growth and the descending workforce which will cause the demand for foreign labour to increase. Meanwhile, Chinese workers will require a higher salary as their labour becomes insufficient. As one company points out *"the wages in China have been raised by 8-10 percent in recent years"* (Case E).

Political challenges in China

According to the empirical studies, the Chinese government is struggling with bribery and corruption within the political system. China is ranked as the seventy-eighth most corrupted country, while Denmark is ranked as one of the less corrupted countries (Bertelsen, 2012). According to an international report in 2009, there is an annual abuse of more than 180 billion dollars within China's political system (Bertelsen, 2012). This great number has been brought to the public's attention, which have created a certain amount of dissatisfaction in the Chinese society towards the political leaders.

The former president Hu Jintao announced in one of his speeches that the problem regarding corruption was not taken seriously. He talks about the concept "Walk the Talk/Talk the Walk", which underlines how many leaders talk a lot about how to take care of a problem, but few actually do something about it. In China this can be a challenge because too many important leaders speak about doing something for the country's problems and issues, but several times it is not followed up on (Hansen & Eiberg 2012).

In China bribery is often spoken about as one interview pointed out *Money Talks* (Case E). The term underlines the problem with corruption because of the way business payments can be made. 'Money Talks' is a concept that underlines business relations to negotiate with one or another through unregistered money.

In some cases, the political behaviour seems to reflect the way Chinese do business. The Chinese business behaviour also affects how Danish companies want to do business in China. From the empirical studies in China, all interviewed companies dissociate with corruption or bribery at any time. One interview comments on the case of bribery in China*"… as a way of dealing with corruptive activities, foreign companies have in many cases incorporated an anti-bribery program in China*' (Case A).

Another political challenge is the lack of legislation for patent rights in China. Foreign companies are struggling with plagiarism. The copying of products threatens to destroy the brand value, which, for some, has taken decades to build up. The majority of the interviewed companies are aware of the challenge and many experience plagiarism in their industry. It is often smaller Chinese firms, who are the main drivers behind plagiarism. Though there are more organized international networks behind these actions as well. However most of the companies are powerless in bringing the criminals of plagiarism to justice. It is easy to copy a product in China without being punished, as one interview pointed out. *"There is no Interpol like in Europe. When criminals do not get punished, it means they will take higher risks. What is missing is an application of law. Criminals who are brought to justice and convicted for plagiarism can easily start a new production centre in another city. Without any political initiatives to prevent plagiarism, the problem seems to continue in China"* (Case A).

History and religious beliefs seem to play an important role in the way Chinese are doing business. For foreign companies, the first step in creating relationships is to know about Chinese history, but also about the underlying values within the Chinese society. Some characteristics of the historical development have already been pointed out in the previous section. However, some of the underlying values in Chinese business behaviour have not yet been clarified. The studies in China have clarified the fact that traditional Chinese values seem to be highly integrated in the way Chinese are negotiating and doing business overall. Values that are highly connected to the traditional Confucian-style supported by elements within Taoism and Buddhism philosophies.

The characteristics of Chinese business culture

When doing business in China, it is important to understand the construction of China and its culture. There are many issues that have to be taken into account. The Chinese way of doing business differs a lot from the Western despite years of cooperation. It is important to understand that the country is not just one country, but that it is constructed of several parts. These several parts have their own 5 year-plan which underlines the goals and how they would like the future to develop for that exact part of China. When choosing a part of China, it is necessary to understand the chosen part's conditions and goals. It is important to fit into these points to create the best future for one's own business.

Before entering China there are several important characteristics to be aware of besides choosing the right part of China, these are underlined in the next section. The Chinese look upon culture seriously and understanding, or at least trying to understand their culture, is crucial.

Guoqing

As mentioned, Chinese culture differs a lot from Western countries. *Guoqing* is a concept often used in relation to Chinese policy and society – it emphasizes the importance in having an insight in Chinese culture. Furthermore it emphasizes the understanding of the factors about Chinese culture before entering the country.

Generally it is important to create networks, especially when doing business in another country. One company stated *"it is almost impossible to do business in China without contacts"* (Case C). Yeung and Tung differ between *group identification* and *altercasting*, which are two ways to facilitate the transformation process in establishing *guanxi*. *Altercasting* is for non-Chinese investors, which is useable in this study. The purpose of *altercasting* is important to use an intermediary to create *guanxi* (Yeung & Tung 1996, pp. 54-65).

The companies emphasized the differences between China and Denmark. Chinese businesses are more focused on creating close relationships, whereas Danish businesses can be characterized as more transactional oriented. Business in China takes time. Trust is crucial in creating *guanxi*. Therefore patience is necessary for Danish companies in China. However, the way of creating networks in China differs significantly from other markets. Compared to Hall's culture theory the Chinese are strongly polychronic because they always prioritize relations first. Danes have a more monochronic tendency. A key word for Danes is 'time is money', which means they prioritize effectiveness and efficiency.

Doing a favour to another person comes from the word *guan* and is closely related to *guanxi*. Case A points out *"In the West, returning a favour happens more or less immediate. In China, the favour may happen over a long time"*. However, refusing a favour in China will in some cases be seen as impolite, which relies on the Chinese principals of not to 'lose face' (Luo, 1997, p. 44-48).

Guanxi

Guanxi consists of Guan and Xi. Guan means 'A door'. When you are behind the door, you are 'one of us', as a Chinese would say. This underlines the difference of Western and Chinese culture, because the Western people see their networks as an individual network, which means you can have several networks without being dependent on one and another. When you are in a network in China, you are also in a network with your partner's partner. When you are in a *guanxi*, you are accepted from all partners. This supports the meaning of Guan as 'one of us'. Xi means 'To tie something up and extend into a relationship'. Guanxi is also characteristic for maintaining a long-term relationship (Luo, 1997, p. 44-48). *Guanxi* has an impact on how the Chinese interact. *Guanxi* is the Chinese word for network and personal relations. The interviewed companies were all well versed in the importance of *guanxi*. In China, *guanxi* also means an investment in the relationship, it is used to strengthen the relations between companies, persons, etc. The Chinese see it as an advantage to utilize each other's resources. They understand network as an opportunity for sharing knowledge and increasing competitive advantage for different nations and cultures (Luo, 1997, pp. 44-48). According to Gesteland, China is relation-oriented, where trust is important in a collectivistic perspective as the Chinese business culture.

Trust and harmony

Shehui dengji (social status) is an element of Chinese culture that refers to conflict management. Avoiding conflict contributes to maintaining harmony (Graham & Lam, 2004, pp. 42-43). *Renji Hexie* describes interpersonal harmony. Interpersonal harmony requires that social commitments are completed on one's social status within one's *guanxi*. (Graham & Lam, 2004, p. 43) As mentioned above, the companies in China expressed that Danes are more interested in transactions, but this does not appear in Chinese culture because of the importance they put on trustful and close relations. Renji Hexie is important to establish when doing business in China. For the Chinese, trust and harmony are more important than contracts. It explains the difference between monochronic and polychronic cultures. The creation of close relationships takes time and the Chinese are likely to spend a lot of time creating harmony between themselves and their partners. Case D points out Chinese to be interested in doing business with foreign companies. However, it does not mean that you are the preferred partner. *Liangshou zhunbei* is the word for 'two way preparation' – it means, that even if you get applied by the Chinese, then he already has contacted your competitor (Graham & Lam, 2004, p. 45).

In addition to trust, the companies in China pointed out that the Chinese are often suspicious towards foreigners. Therefore it is important to act like one of them and fulfil their needs when doing business with them.

According to Geert Hofstede's dimension; individualism - the Chinese have a score of 20, which means that the culture is highly collectivistic and that they are thinking holistically (Hofstede, 2012a). Holistic thinking means that the Chinese are thinking in groups, and are taking care of themselves and people they have a relation to. Case A sees it as a disadvantage for Danish companies, because of the lack of empathy for others in China. The company expressed the importance in patience when doing business in China.

Face

During this study, throughout interviews with several companies, it became clear that the most humiliating for Chinese people is to 'lose face'. *Mianzi* describes the word 'face', and it is a person's reputation and social standing (Graham & Lam, 2004, p. 48). Chinese and Western management differs a lot, which Chinese employees are much aware of. They are suspicious towards Western managers confronting them in public. According to Hofstede, Danes have a direct communication, whereas China is placed as highly contextual using a lot of nonverbal communication. Chinese employees are more comfortable when having a local manager, because Western managers can weaken their social status (Peng & Tjosvold, 2011, pp. 1032-1036).

As mentioned China is in rapid development and this will have an impact on the future in China.

Future China

China is in a kind of transformation. Building innovative skills is on the agenda. China wants to be an innovative country according to the five-year plan. The Chinese government wants Chinese companies to move up the value curve and expand globally. This is also the case if China wants to ensure long-term growth. According to the empirical studies there is a mismatch between the political agenda and the behaviour of Chinese people. To a large extent, the basic capacity for Research and Development (R&D) is missing. A traditional R&D process in China is to improve already existing products. It means Chinese are still relatively challenged in inventing new products. Thus, the Chinese government is trying to encourage the Chinese population to become entrepreneurs through political initiatives. The expectations are clear. China is moving from being a preferable low-cost production to include R&D activities. However, the transformation has affected the wages in China. Within five years the Chinese will no longer be as competitive on price as they are today, especially in the coastal regions like Shanghai and Beijing. Thus, it may only be beneficial if companies want to penetrate the Chinese market and thereby be close to the customers.

Doing R&D in China

In response, many multinational companies have made China one of their priority locations for R&D centres, despite cultural difficulties such as language and Intellectual Property Rights (IPR) problems. However, there are some advantages of doing R&D in China. One of the main reasons lies in the growing middle class in China. The purchasing power of the middle class will increase dramatically within a few years. In the light of this development, costs of hiring engineers and researchers will go up.

Doing R&D in China also has the advantage of being closer to the market and consumers. Companies can invent adapted products that meet Chinese demands more easily. They can do this by hiring Chinese staff members, who have a closer relationship to the local consumers. Besides, there are investment incentives such as tax rebates and faster approval, and companies are seen as a more committed, trustworthy and long-term partner by the Chinese government and the public. Foreign R&D centres can also help their companies establish relationships with important Chinese partners. Partnerships with universities are valuable to companies' R&D potential due to the domestic talent pool. Still, foreign companies might be keeping key innovation at home because abuse can occur. However, foreign companies have to be aware of the basic laws and regulations in China. Every business' behaviour is governed by laws. For instance IPR is important to a company's core competitiveness. Thus, effective IPR protection at R&D centres where IPR is developed is essentially considered an increasing Chinese high-tech culture.

Chinese management

Despite a massive workforce, qualities as leadership, creativity and service have for long time been in short supply in China. The number of Chinese who return to China after studying or working abroad is going to rise significantly in the years ahead, and they have these qualities. Previously, many Chinese who studied or worked abroad also stayed there because the opportunities in China were limited. According to the empirical study, a lot of Chinese have been expats for five to ten years in areas like the United States and Europe and they are of interest because they have explored and copied some of the Western management skills. Though, their behaviour still carries out the fundamental values of Chinese culture.

In that perspective, many Chinese are now starting to return to China due to the economic growth and job opportunities. The government offers favourable policies on areas like tax regulations to students who have studied abroad and are highly educated. It is also why foreign companies should develop an explicit government relationship management strategy to try to level the playing field, in order for the Chinese companies to increasingly have Chinese leaders with experience in managing international organizations.

Some of the interviews in China predict great opportunities and challenges in China. For instance, the next Chinese generation will be aligned with the Western management style in general. The new generation will have a good grasp of the English language. They will have the capacity to build bridges much stronger than the Chinese are capable of doing today. This will have an influence on how the international companies organize and manage in China and as a result the expats will properly disappear. The expats, whom are still in China in five to ten years, will be those related to innovation.

E-commerce

The use of the Internet is being integrated faster in China than anywhere else on earth. The e-commerce market in China will continue to evolve, where the prospect is to become the world's largest in 2015 (Silverstein et al., 2012).

According to the empirical studies, the e-commerce creates great opportunities for the companies. It will create a faster access in order to reach the online consumer. Currently, China has 193 million online shoppers. By 2015, the Chinese will be the biggest e-shoppers in the world. There will be 356 million Chinese shopping online, and they will spend more than $360 billion. Half the Chinese population will have access to the Internet in three years, which will be twice as many as in the United States and Japan together (Silverstein et al., 2012).

However, there are obstacles. There are a number of linguistic, cultural and legal barriers, combined with the Western companies' lack of in-depth knowledge of the Chinese online consumption pattern. Because the Chinese market and its consumers differ completely from most of the Western markets, the Western companies need to know their target group.

Furthermore, foreign companies face governmental obstacles as well. The government is known for its "Great Firewall", where access to certain foreign websites is prohibited. For instance, the government blocks social media like Facebook and Twitter. However, there are national social media sites.

China becomes individualized

The degree of individualism in China is dependent on the evolution of society and social interaction. Individualism is defined by the individual's ability to make independent choices and the relation to education, democracy and the values that defined the local or global culture. In line with China's growing prosperity, it is interesting to consider the way the Chinese business behaviour is going to change. As mentioned, the Chinese have a high score of collectivism. However the Chinese are not always appropriate for ridge hierarchies, when trying to build an innovative society. In the past years, Chinese business people have travelled abroad and have experienced the impact from the Western individualism. In that case it has an effect on China which slowly becomes more individualized (Kruse, 2012).

Recommendations

During our study in China we were attentive of several elements that are important for Danish companies when doing business in China.

Government and five-year plan

It was clarified that the government has an impact on business in China. The government decides and manages everything. In the light of government role, there are some key aspects that must be taken into account for companies to become interesting. One company stated *"money talks"* in China. Foreign products and services must contribute to further growth and improvement for the Chinese society. As one interview pointed out *"The Chinese government puts a lot of economic resources in technology and new energy solutions"* (Case B).

The five-year plan due to the government emphasizes several improvements in different regions and new initiatives that the governments are planning to perform. This five-year plan can help Danish companies be aware of which improvements or initiatives are coming in the concerning regions. Therefore it is important that companies have a clear plan for which region to enter, because China is not one China, it is seen as a country with different regions.

Clear strategy

China is a minefield for companies. The opportunities in the country are huge, but so are the pitfalls. China requires great preparation and patience before the investment is recouped. In some cases, failures are caused by a lack of understanding of China. One interview pointed out *"it is important to be prepared and never lose focus of what you want"* (Case C).

Furthermore, companies must be presence at all time in China. Jørgen Mads Clausen, chairman of Danfoss, points out that it is not enough to visit China a couple of times. A well-prepared strategy is needed; including examining the penetration barriers and opportunities in China (Nymark, 2012).

Findings in this study reveal the importance of Chinese culture in a business relationship. Case B states that long-term planning does not exist in China. The cause might be related to the rapid growth in China. Danish companies must be flexible in the organizational structure and decision process. Meanwhile, the Chinese business is rapidly moving and it creates an inequality for what is ethical right to do and what is not.

Control mechanism

One interview pointed out, companies cannot expect to organize their way out in China. Companies must have the ability to adapt. To gain control of the Chinese workers, managers also need to be more operational in China compared to the West as pointed out in one interview *"...Because of the lack of accuracy, CEO members becomes much more operational in China than in other places. Chinese are very creative, but the challenge for managers is to use their creativeness for the sake of the company and not for their own interest. That is a managing thing"* (Case A). Without a control mechanism installed in China, Chinese will do what they think is right and this is not always beneficial for the business. *"This goes through the whole Chinese society. You have to be critical and direct in terms of management"* (Case A). Companies need to repeat rules to keep business activities in line. Companies have to be alert and setting rules that are respected when starting business in China.

How to build *guanxi*

The study in China emphasized the importance of *guanxi*, but how to build *guanxi* is not as easy as it seems. Trust is crucial for the creation of guanxi. Trust is often created through social events. One interview pointed out *"you need to be more socialized with people in China than you normally would be in the West, to become successful".*

Furthermore, the study reveals that the Danish consulate in Shanghai and the Danish embassy in Beijing offer support to Danish companies. The consulate and the Danish embassy may provide valuable information on how to enter the Chinese market. For some companies, it might be the gate to new potential partners in China, and also the access to the Chinese market.

Reflection

Chinas financial transformation has developed within 30 years. In Europe it took more than 100 years to build its financial platform and sets of values. China is still in a learning process, where Europe and America can be expressed as the teachers. In Europe, there are some underlying values of how to do business across national borders. These underlying values are also supported by national and international legal regulations within Europe. In China, the underlined values are blurred combined with the lack of a legal system. This may affect the way Chinese are doing business and may be the case in terms of ethical boundaries. In some cases, it might be unfair to expect that Chinese people know what is right or wrong. How do Chinese know the ethical boundaries, when no one has ever told them how to do things?

Chinas history and development may take great responsibility for why a lot of Western companies perceive Chinese behaviour as unpredictable and with a great lack of all credibility. Some would argue that the consequences of the communist regime have led to corruption and injustice, where people were used to do things the government felt was right. Others would argue that the consequences of the open economy have led to a greater capitalistic temptation, where the cultural traditions of China seem to disappear due to the impact of cultural globalization. Some interviewed companies have experienced a number of incidents, where managers in the company had to be replaced due to corruption. Corruption and bribery seems to be an integral part of the political system and Chinese society as a whole. The Chinese government can ignore these destructive mechanisms to affect Chinas growth, image and power.

For China, the communist approach might be beneficial in terms of flexibility and making quick decisions due to the centralized political structure. The growth of China lies very much on (few) decision makers within the Central committee of the Communist party. Inspired by Mao Zedong, Chinas growth still depends on the five-year plan. The five-year plan has its advantage and challenges. For both national and foreign companies, the five-year plan can provide certainty in terms of development on the shorter run. However, in the long run the direction is more uncertain. The direction of China and the Chinese government may become more unstable and unpredictable due to rapid changing markets, which may affect the way of doing business in China.

To some extent, China still becomes a paradox. On one hand, there is a great admiration when it comes to the ability to produce wealth to a middle class that now represents more than 200 million Chinese and is achieved only within 30 years. On the other hand, it can be questioned whether the Chinese economy is in its full expression as long as there is no democratic mechanism placed in the political system. Some are questioning Chinas ability to maintain the political control and structure, when the economy seems to become more globalized. Furthermore, it can be questioned whether China has the ability and leadership to become the world's most powerful nation, when the Chinese society still is characterized as unorganized and socially divided.

Conclusion

The research in this study reveals Chinese behaviour to be a mix of old Chinese traditions and the economic and political transformation in the last century. Firstly, the use of Chinese traditions is mainly shown in the Confucian style, which includes the concepts of *guoqing* and *guanxi*. Secondly, the Chinese search for stability and harmony in life relies on cultural traditions within the philosophy of Taoism. Thirdly, the Chinese way of enduring hardship and suffering is inspired by some of the principles in the Buddhist mind-set.

Furthermore, the transformation of Chinas society can be seen as a consequence of political changing led by Mao Zedong 1949 and economic reforms in 1978 by Deng Xiaoping. For many Chinese, Mao is still the symbol of great leadership and control, who transformed China into a major world power. Others claim Mao to cause the death of more than 17 million people during his communist regime. However, the rapid growth of Chinese society may honour Deng Xiaoping and the economic transformation which opened China to the world.

Even though China has become a powerful actor to the global economy, the country is still struggling with corruption and other destructive mechanisms within its political system. These mechanisms are influencing the Chinese business behaviour as well.

Guanxi is one of the essential aspects in Chinese business culture. The companies in this study requested all foreign companies to face the importance of *guanxi*. Guanxi can also be seen as closely related to the level of trust and the concept of not losing face. The Chinese concept of lose face must be avoided to create network and personal relationship. These three aspects are essential in describing Chinese business culture. These aspects differ from Western companies, which seem to be more transactional in their negotiating behaviour rather than building up relationships first. In relation to that, trust appears to be important.

In some cases, Chinese think someone is trying to cheat them. This reflects on Chinese behaviour, where actions will more likely be of own interest rather than what is best for the company. Therefore, a control mechanism is crucial to avoid business failure. To gain control of the Chinese workers, managers need to be more operational in China compared to the West. Furthermore, Companies need to repeat rules to keep business activities in line. Companies have to be alert and setting rules that are respected when starting business in China. China is going to change rapidly. China will become attractive for a number of foreign companies due to the following factors.

First of all China will focus on innovation; the Chinese government encourages domestic and foreign companies to invest in R&D in China and will be more cooperative than in the past.

Secondly, China's e-commerce market will develop significantly as well. Already in 2015, the Chinese e-commerce market will be the world's largest. There will be 356 million Chinese shopping online. So if foreign companies are able to understand and adapt to the Chinese online consumption pattern, they will have all the opportunities to become successful.

Finally, the Chinese education system is being fast developed, thus more people will achieve a higher level of educational skills than in the past. About 83 million Chinese will, over the next 10 years, take a college degree. At the same time, the labour market will still be a relatively low-cost-market. So economically China will still be attractive.

The Chinese demand will increase as the economy grows. Thus, production of goods and services can further push the Chinese economy's growth. The Chinese consumption market will become more efficient and industries will grow even faster than before. Still, the corruption in the Chinese government remains a threat to China's economic development as well as bribery in the Chinese business culture.

CHAPTER 3

Offshoring to China, drivers and barriers

Anna-Sophia Lauritzen, Janni Grouleff Nielsen, Sisse Levi Hansen, Kim Mandrup Hansen and Martin Haugegaard

Abstract

The purpose of this chapter is to provide an insight into the challenges of operating a production facility or other units in China. Following, there will be a discussion of ways to overcome these challenges based on empirical findings during the study. The experience of successfully established Danish companies in China is most useful in meeting the challenges of offshoring. The question of strategic planning versus learning by doing will be applied, as it is central to reduce fixed costs prior to the offshoring process avoiding sunk costs. The study will rely on first-hand experience of operating in China.

Introduction

Diminishing borders are adding increasing pressure on companies to become more international and even global in their operations. This offers possibilities as well as threats, which can be utilized. To ensure the survival of the company, one must focus on the core competencies of the company and thereby obtain sustainable competitive advantages vis-á-vis competitors (Arlbjørn et al., 2010). Focusing on core competencies means to only engage in those activities in which the company has an advantage over its competitors and outsource the remaining activities to external partners. This can cause loss of control and coordination, which can cancel out the obtained benefits of a specialization strategy. A way to reduce these risks is to offshore instead of outsourcing, where the control is still in the hands of the company, but the function in question has been relocated to a different country. The distance between the company and the relocated function can cause some increased costs, which must be less than the benefits of maintaining control and coordination to ensure a successful offshoring (Dunning in Arlbjørn & Lüthje, 2012).

For a Danish company, there are some clear advantages by offshoring to China. The wages are lower than in Denmark in spite of recently increasing Chinese wages, and the work mentality of the workforce allows for high efficiency in production units. These advantages can also be obtained by locating a function in Eastern Europe, so why China? China's rapid development over the past many decades has increased the wealth of the country and thereby the living standard of the population causing increased consumption and an expanding market. The rise in living standards, and thereby wages of the workforce, has decreased the cost benefits of operating in China, which means that it is no longer enough to only exploit the low wages of the Chinese workforce (Arlbjørn et al., 2010; case company B and C). Between this and the expanding Chinese market, a shift has occurred causing the benefits from being in China to become market driven instead of resource driven (de Wit & Meyer, 2010). The main driver for offshoring to China should then be to sell products in the Chinese market. In fact, one of the case companies in this study experienced shipping a large percentage of the Danish production to China and not so large a percentage from the Chinese production to Denmark (Case Company C). This shows that the Chinese market is expanding more rapidly than the production facilities of the Danish case company in China.

In order to operate successfully in China, adaptation is required. The cultural, political, technological and economic differences make it difficult to operate a Western company in China with no regard to these differences. The challenges of adapting to the Chinese market are many and difficult to overcome, which is why it is important to make preparations prior to offshoring, to be flexible and ready to change when facing new unforeseen challenges when operating in China and to draw on the experience made by others in order to avoid unforeseen challenges. This brings us to the main purpose of this chapter; to summarize the experiences made by Danish companies when operating in China, by exemplifying ways to meet the found challenges. Knowing the purpose of having a production unit in China answers the question why but raises the question how. The purpose of this chapter is to answer the following questions:

1. *What are the challenges of operating in China?*

2. *How can one meet the challenges of operating in China?*
3. *Should a company plan everything before offshoring or learn as they go along?*

These research questions seek to offer a practical approach for Danish companies who wish to enter the Chinese market and claim the benefits hereof.

The following section describes the methodology for collecting and using the empirical data that form the substance of the analysis. Then a section follows on the theoretical framework for analysing the collected data. Hereafter the analytical section follows, where the collected data is treated. Finally, the answers to the research questions are summarized in the conclusion.

Methodology

The content of this chapter is the result of a process containing a literature review, a collection and treatment of data from the case companies and an analysis and forming of the conclusion.

METHODOLOGY		
Stage 1 - Before	Stage 2 - In China	Stage 3 - After
– Literature review	– Collection of data	– Interpretation
– Theoretical framework	– Coding	– Analysis
		– Conslusion

Table 3.1: Methodological stages
Source: Own creation

Literature review

The literature review contained a search for documents relevant to the research questions in order to discover relevant theories and models for describing some of the already known challenges of offshoring. These challenges were then cross-referenced to those challenges found during the study of the empirical data. The literature review resulted in a set of challenges which were kept in mind during the empirical study. The collection of empirical data supported some of the challenges found in the literature review while others were not expected and new to the literature.

Collection of data

The collection of data was carried out over a four-day period, interviewing two companies a day. These separate case studies relied on the same interview guide based on theories from the literature review to increase comparability in the study, thus allowing to rate the challenges in ascending order, based on number of appearances.

Case study

The collection of data took place in the form of a case study, where seven separate Danish companies and one joint venture between a Danish and a Chinese company were interviewed in depth through a semi-structured approach. The case study made it possible to collect hands-on experience from relevant employees in offshored units of Danish companies. The advantages of the case study allow the researcher to collect complex data within a specific context and a specific area of expertise. It also gives the opportunity to influence the data collection process due to the presence of the researcher. This, however, might also be a disadvantage if not considered during the formulation of the interview guide and might cause biases in the data. The advantages of the case study fall great in line with the purpose of this chapter, namely to exemplify how challenges have been met in real life situations (Bryman & Bell, 2011).

The companies interviewed remain anonymous in the case study. This gives the companies in question more freedom to divulge sensitive information critical to the study. This increases the reliability of the study and helps increase the range of the use of the study (Yin in Haug & Heldbjerg, 2011). The case companies will be coded as case company A-B-C-D-E-F-G-H.

The case study will be formed as an abductive research because the study, prior to the empirical study, generates a framework of challenges found in the literature review. This is then tested in the empirical findings and supplemented by challenges found in the empirical study, which were not specifically mentioned in the literature.

In the Theoretical Reflections section, eight main challenges were found mentioned in the literature and listed in Table 3.3. These were then held against the challenges found in the empirical study and a grouping of the challenges was made, resulting in five main challenges listed in Table 3.4. The grouping was made to ease the reading of the chapter.

Company description

The companies in the study are primarily large Danish companies with divisions in China. One joint venture with a Chinese company was also included in the study. The main characteristics of these companies are:

1. They are well established in their respective businesses
2. They have been in existence for a long time
3. They all target the premium segment in their respective businesses
4. They apply a Scandinavian leadership style

These characteristics are significant in understanding the culture of the companies. This Western culture often conflicts with the Chinese culture causing many of the challenges discovered during this study. The fact that they are well established, "old" companies can be both a good and a bad thing. On one side, there are some scale advantages to being a large well-established company. On the other hand, a large (slow) company may not be as flexible, responsive or innovative as smaller, less established companies (de Wit & Meyer, 2010). Figure 3.1 shows the relationship between the case companies and their competitors. This relationship was generally applicable in all case companies. The circles in the figure represent the actors in the Chinese market. The circle in the low segment represents the Chinese companies, and the circle in the premium segment represents the Danish case companies. The movements seen in the figure from premium and low to mid segment represent the movement in the market. Several case companies described how Chinese competitive companies have improved some of their products moving them towards the mid segment forcing the case companies to penetrate this segment as well in order to maintain their competitive advantages and market shares. Another advantage of entering this mid-market is the fact that this market is increasing in relative size due to the increase in living standards, which all of the case companies' experience. Access to the mid-market was created by acquisition of Chinese or American companies (case company B), who supplied the mid-market, and investing capital in these companies to strengthen the position in the mid-market. This solution was chosen to avoid loss of brand quality in their premium products and to avoid association between the two brands.

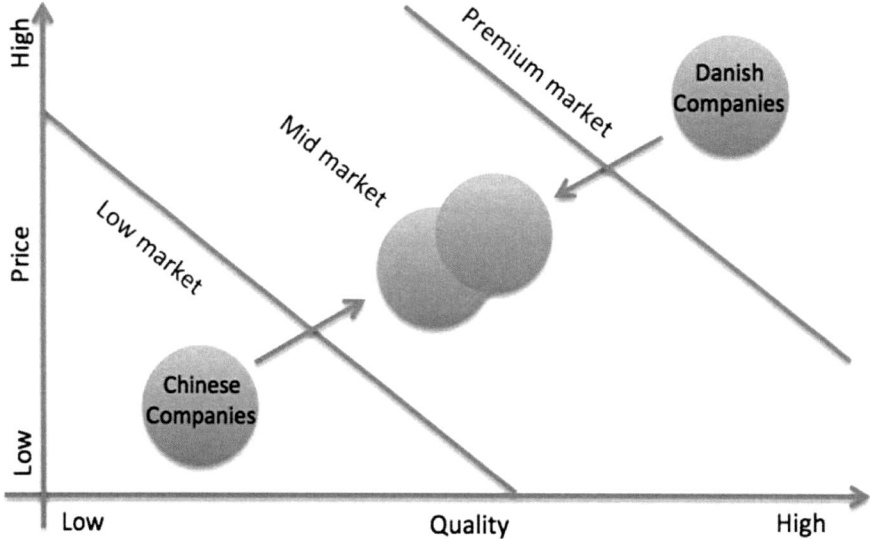

Figure 3.1: The Chinese Market
Source: Own creation based on case company B and G

The last characteristic concerning the Scandinavian leadership style is significant in that it exemplifies the cultural difference between China and Denmark. The case companies in this study implements a Scandinavian leadership style thus staying true to the corporate culture and strategy of the company (case company B, C, D and G). The Scandinavian leadership style comprises the following (Buus, 2004):

- Respect for the individual
- A holistic, humanistic and value-based approach with a multiple stakeholder focus
- Flat and non-bureaucratic organizations with a high degree of devolved responsibility and accountability
- Trust, care and concern as key values

The selection of case companies in this study gives the study a one-sided perspective. It only allows the reader to view the challenges of doing business in China from a Danish company's perspective. This is in line with the purpose of the chapter, namely to give Danish companies, who wish to become aware of some of the challenges met when offshoring, the solutions created by other successful Danish companies.

Theoretical reflections

Definitions

When deciding on a sourcing strategy, it is important to distinguish between which products/components to produce inside the company (make) and which to purchase from external partners in the network (buy). This is a matter of core competences, as it is important to maintain the control over the most crucial processes influencing the competitive advantage of the company.

Outsourcing

Outsourcing can be defined in two ways: The first concerns what is sourced from outside the company, and the second is the process of moving activities to external partners (Arlbjørn et al., 2010 p. 240). Common for both definitions is that the ownership, and thereby control of the activity, lies with the external company. In this chapter, the distinction between outsourcing and offshoring is made on basis of the second definition.

Offshoring

As with outsourcing, offshoring can be defined either as that of having a unit or function located in another country or the process of relocating a unit or function from the domestic to a foreign country (Arlbjørn et al., 2010, p. 240). In this chapter, the second definition is applied, thereby moving focus from the process of closing down operations and setting them up in a foreign country to operating in the foreign country after having set up the function.

Strategic formation

The purpose of this chapter is, as mentioned, to bring insight to companies considering offshoring a production unit (or other units) to China. It was therefore deemed necessary to bring the aspect of strategic formation into the discussion. Should a company plan everything before offshoring, or is it better to learn as you go along?

The complexity of a problem - Tame and Wicked problems

The complexity of a problem or a decision is a central point for some theorists' discussion about the paradox of deliberateness and emergentness. The decision of whether to offshore or not can be seen as a complex wicked problem. A wicked problem is characterised by being complicated, interconnected with other problems and filled with uncertainty. In contrast to a wicked problem, a tame problem is defined as having a well-defined goal, the solution can be tested and the problem may repeat itself many times. J. Quinn among others argues that a deliberate approach only works on tame problems because strategists rarely have the luxury of using generic solutions to solve strategic problems (de Wit & Meyer, 2010).

The paradox of Deliberateness and Emergentness

The paradox of Deliberateness and Emergentness is all about how the process of strategy formation takes place in organisations. Theorists define strategy in many different ways, which naturally causes different opinions of how "strategy should be made". A realized strategy can be formed in two very different ways – it can either start with a deliberate strategy that leads to the realized strategy or it can be formed over time as an emergent strategy (de Wit & Meyer, 2010).

Figure 3.2 graphically illustrates the two different ways in which the deliberate and emergent strategies become the realized strategy.

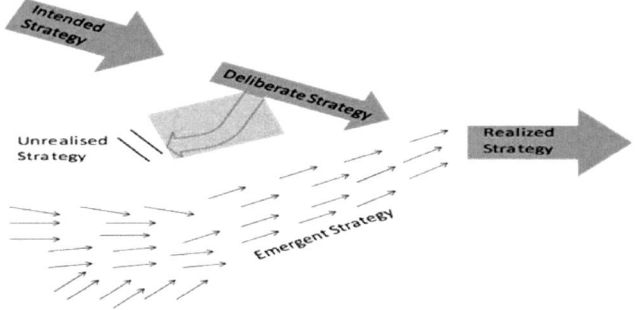

Figure 3.2: Forms of strategy
Source: de Wit & Meyer (2010, p. 114)

The two paradoxes cause two different perspectives to arise amongst theorists. The Deliberateness paradox forms the "Strategic Planning" perspective, and the Emergentness paradox forms the "Strategic

Incrementalism" perspective. Direction, commitment, coordination, optimization and programming are all characteristics for the strategic planning perspective. The strategic incrementalism strategy is on the other hand characterised by learning, experimenting, sense-making and reflecting. The incrementalism perspective is not about *figuring out* but more about *finding out* the strategy.

Table 3.2 illustrates the continuums of the key factors for the strategic planning perspective and the strategic incrementalism perspective.

	STRATEGIC PLANNING PERSPECTIVE	STRATEGIC INCREMENTALISM PERSPECTIVE
Emphasis on	Deliberateness over emergence	Emergence over deliberateness
Nature of strategy	Intentionalle designed	Gradually shaped
Nature of formation	Figuring out	Finding out
View of future	Forecast and anticipate	Partially unknown and unpredictable
Posture towards the future	Make commitments, prepare	Postpone commitments, remail flexible
Formation process	Formally structured and comprehensive	Unstructured and fragmented
Formation process steps	First think, then act	Thinking and acting intertwined
Decision-making	Hierarchical	Dispersed
Decision-making focus	Optimal ressource allocation and coordination	Experimentation and parallel initiatives
Implementation focused on	Programming (organizational effiency)	Learning (organizational development)
Strategic change	Implemented top-down	Requires broad cultural and cognitive shifts

Table 3.2: Strategic planning versus strategic incrementalism perspective
Source: de Wit and Meyer (2010, p. 128)

Challenges for offshoring in the literature

In the literature review, we have found eight main challenges that can harm companies who wish to do business in China. A lot of the literature review is written about outsourcing, but because many of the factors are caused by the specific country and culture instead of dependent on companies' globalization strategy, we found that these factors are relevant when studying offshoring. These barriers can be seen when companies outsource as well as offshore. In the following table, some of the main challenges are listed by authors.

	LOSS OF CONTROL	LOSS OF CRITICAL SKILLS (QUALITY PROBLEM)	LOSS OF FLEX-IBILITY (INCREASED LEAD-TIME)	HIDDEN COSTS	CULTURE	TACIT KNOW-LEDGE	INVENTORY COSTS / TRANSPOR-TATION	COMMUNI-CATION BARRIERS
Arlbjørn Lüthje (2012)	√	√	√	√	√	√	√	√
Lau and Zhang (2006)	√	√	√	√	√			√
Holweg et al (2011)	√	√	√	√		√	√	√
Gray et al (2011)	√	√	√	√	√			√
Handfield (1994)			√	√	√		√	√
Kinkel (2012)		√	√					

Table 3.3: Main challenges for outsourcing and offshoring listed by different authors
Source: Own creation

Loss of control

It can be more difficult for a Danish company to operate an offshored department in China, than to manage the same department in Denmark, due to increasing location complexity (Arlbjørn et al., 2010, p. 240). It may be caused by geographic distance from corporate headquarters in Denmark, which increases the requirements of the coordination activities. If the geographical distance is large enough, the time difference also becomes a challenge, making basic communication difficult to manage properly.

Loss of critical skills

When operating a unit/function in a foreign country, some skills might not be utilized due to that the headquarter is less involved in the operation. The expert knowledge is not so readily available, causing quality challenges. Furthermore, if the operating team, the processes, blueprints and operations equipment are not relocated as well or at least duplicated in the foreign location, some important knowledge may be lost, causing quality or even simple operation challenges. Gray et al. (2011) exemplify cases where these losses of critical skills have been so severe that the company was forced to relocate the function/unit back to the domestic country, causing great financial losses.

Loss of flexibility

Having a production in a foreign country can slow down the coordination activities and thereby decreasing the flexibility/responsiveness of the company. Furthermore, the shipping of products from China to the rest of the world (mainly the Western part) requires a very long lead-time by sea, due to high transportation cost by air or road. This means that for six-eight weeks there is nothing you can do about the products already shipped (Handfield, 1994; case company B, D). Due to this, a company can suffer severely under the long lead-time if it is a company that differentiates itself from its competitors on this parameter (Porter, 1985). Also, if the company retains the R&D department of the company in the domestic country, the flexibility suffers due to lack of coordinating abilities between the R&D department and the production unit. Besides, challenges concerning transfer of knowledge about a new product from the R&D department to the production unit (blueprints, setups, etc.) may cause longer time-to-market, lowering flexibility/responsiveness to the changing market conditions (Heizer & Render, 2011). Last but not least, cooperation with suppliers and customers can be compromised if the market is located at a great geographical distance from the production facility, because coordination between these is critical when supplying the market. So, when offshoring the production of only a part of the finished product, loss of flexibility might occur when shipments of components from Denmark create a bottleneck.

Hidden cost

These costs include those, which are not related to the actual supply chain operation, but instead originate from the wider business environment. It can be currency fluctuations, political (in)stability, changing prices for e.g. energy and water, regulatory framework, taxes, duties, infrastructure, and corruption. It is in general very difficult to predict these costs (Lau & Zhang, 2006, p. 786). This challenge is particularly important when offshoring, because the Danish companies offshoring a production unit to China (or any other country) may not be particularly well informed about the local regulations of the above mentioned hidden costs.

Culture

The cultural aspect of offshoring is important in all activities in the supply chain. It is vital to know the culture of your suppliers and possible suppliers in order to know how to act and maybe especially bargain with your suppliers. On the downstream side, it is also critical to have an understanding of the local tacit knowledge culture to provide the most profitable products and avoid failures in the market place. Furthermore, knowing the culture in the operation of the offshored unit is of eminent importance when for example hiring the workforce and understanding the communication, values and norms in the department. The cultural aspect as a challenge when operating in a foreign country will not be discussed at length in this chapter, as it is discussed in another chapter concerning culture.

Tacit knowledge

This challenge is more visible in the task of outsourcing, but may also be valuable to be aware of when offshoring. Tacit knowledge concerns the knowledge which lies with the employees of the company. It is not substantialised in any form and will be lost when reducing staff. Tacit knowledge is aggregated over time as the employees move along the learning curve. The more complex a product or process is, the longer time it takes to build this knowledge and the more costly it will be to re-establish it once lost. Examples of are technical knowhow and relations between employees, department or even units. These forms of knowledge may cause severe setbacks if lost, and therefore it is important *"…to have the processes in control before they are outsourced. Otherwise you are just exporting problems"* (Arlbjørn & Lüthje, 2012). This is mostly relevant when outsourcing, but it may be difficult for a company to move an entire production unit to a foreign country and move all employees with it.

Inventory/transportation cost

First, inventory costs can be expected to increase when locating a production unit in a foreign country, when exporting the produced goods back to the domestic country. This is because of the longer lead-time requiring larger inventories to cope with the fluctuations/uncertainty in demand. Second, the transportation cost will also increase when exporting from the foreign country because of the increased distance to the domestic market.

Communication barriers

It is more difficult to communicate in another language and it can create misunderstandings. It is not only the language that can create problems. Also differences in culture can make it more difficult to communicate and at worst create mistrust between the involved parties. The distance can be a communication barrier because a lot of the communication has to be in writing or by phone instead of face to face, and also the communication setup and maintenance may be very costly. Even though the department in China is Danish owned, it does not mean that there are exclusively Danish people on the location. This means that the Danish headquarter has to talk with their employees in another language and with another cultural background.

The above-mentioned challenges will in the subsequent section be analysed in accordance with the empirical findings made. The next section also includes a set of challenges met in the empirical study, which were not found in the literature review.

Empirical findings

Challenges of offshoring in the empirical findings

The empirical study was performed on the basis of the challenges found in the literature review. However, the empirical study presented a different grouping of challenges, which were categorized into four topics of challenges for offshoring to China: loss of critical skills, flexibility, hidden costs, and culture. These four challenges is a result of a grouping of the eight challenges found in the literature review, as mentioned earlier. Furthermore, strategy has been added, resulting in five challenges. The degree to which preparations can be made prior to the offshoring process was also an important aspect of the study. In Table 3.4, some characteristics associated with the challenges are presented, and in the following sections each challenge will be analysed, exemplified and presented for a possible solution for how to deal with it based on experiences made by the case companies.

LOSS OF CRITICAL SKILLS	FLEXIBILTY	HIDDEN COSTS (PEST)	CULTURE	STRATEGY
Tacit knowledge	Leadtime	Political	Communication	Deliberate - Emergent
Quality	Costs, stock	- Infrastructure	One child policy	Local - Global
	R&D	- 5 year plan and local government	Face	
		Economic	Trust	
		- Currency	Supplier	
		Socio Cultural	Copy-cats	
		- Corruption	Guanxi	
		Technological		
		- Unavailability		
		- Internet payment		

Table 3.4: Main challenges for offshoring to China
Source: Own creation

For all challenges it can be acknowledged that the case companies have partly confirmed the theory and partly generated new knowledge for overcoming challenges of offshoring to China.

The following section deals with the challenges loss of critical skills and flexibility. The characteristic of these challenges is that they occur within the supply chain and can to some degree be prepared for by planning and preparation before engaging in activities concerning offshoring.

Challenge: Loss of critical skills

Tacit knowledge

The challenge of tacit knowledge was experienced by case company B and G. They found it to be too expensive to have Danish leaders in China, because the Danish leaders were paid a Danish salary, making them more costly than a Chinese employee. This was experienced by almost all case companies, who experienced high costs to white collar wages, because Danish leaders in China received Danish wages (case company B, D, G). This means that some of the tacit knowledge from Danish white collars is lost when offshoring. Another challenge was a high job rotation ratio among blue-collar workers. The reason for this is the fact that many workers arrive to the major cities from the provinces of mid-China to work temporarily and then return home to their families. This challenge is especially significant in the case companies because of the complexity and quality standard of the premium products they produce. Furthermore, Chinese workers have a hard-work mentality and focus on net wages, which means that a worker might receive a higher wage per hour from a Danish company, but because the Danish company employs Chinese people to work less hours per week than a Chinese company would, the worker might switch to another job with a lower hourly wage but longer work hours so as to increase the net wage (case company B, C, D, E, F, G).

Tacit knowledge: Solutions

Some of the solutions found to the above mentioned problems concerning loss of tacit knowledge were to educate and train Chinese workers in accordance with Danish culture and knowledge from the Danish headquarter in order to transfer knowledge to the Chinese department without having expensive Danish employees there (case company C). A solution to the problem concerning job rotation was found in the family mentality of the Chinese people. The parents and grandparents have a high degree of influence on the children's lives. Therefore the case companies involve the parents in their children's day-to-day life by showing them around the factory, sending Christmas cards and arranging "family days" (case company B, C, D, F, G). A few incidents of employees staying with the case company, instead of taking another job with a competitor, because his parents liked the case company and its treatment of their son, were given as examples. Furthermore, two case companies implemented bonuses for achieving goals, because of the motivational effect, which is significant in China. These initiatives to secure a capable workforce are part of the Scandinavian leadership style, which is implemented in the entire concern. Other factors influencing job retention were such as air-conditioning, safety equipment and free meals at the work place.

Quality

The Chinese mentality concerning quality was described shortly to us as "good enough". This is a cultural mind-set, which does not pressure the Chinese to produce products of high quality, as many Western companies are known for. This is a challenge for Danish companies operating in China, because more focus is needed to ensure the quality of the produced goods. This may be an expression of the low cost attitude that the Chinese are known for. The general idea is that low cost means low quality or functionality. This challenge is especially important for some of the case companies who produce equipment used in food and pharmaceutical processing industries, where the error margin has to be very low. It is also important for many other companies because more and more customers in China seek high quality products – including the Chinese government. An example of this was one case company experiencing a customer wishing to only buy products from the Danish department, and did not care that the products actually were produced in China and then shipped back to Denmark for approval. This was because of the quality perceived when buying from Denmark. Another aspect to the quality challenge is the working hours. Having Chinese workers working around the clock means greater risk of errors and thereby loss of quality (case company F).

Quality: Solutions

One of the possible solutions to reducing errors in the production processes is to apply several 100 % tests. These tests on component level are performed at several stages during the production and finally right before shipment to ensure as few errors as possible (case company D). Another solution to reduce errors was to implement restrictions on the employees regarding the number of hours per week they are allowed to work, as mentioned in the above section. This should help securing routinized employees and increase the skill level of each employee performing a specific task. However, this restriction may cause some employees to quit their jobs for another job, where they can work longer hours. But if a company is successful in keeping their employees within the company (e.g. through retention programs such as those implemented by case company B or through increase in employees' job satisfaction as attempted by implementing a Scandinavian leadership style), the negative effect of the restrictions can be modified.

Challenge: Flexibility

Lead-time

The challenge found in the literature review concerning lead-time was confirmed during the case study. The fact that China is located at a great geographical distance means long delivery times as mentioned earlier. Some of the case companies experienced challenges when facing a delivery time of six-eight weeks. An example was given of a wrong shipment being made, and when the first container was opened in Denmark, the mistake was discovered, but because of the long delivery, wrong deliveries would keep on arriving for the next 6-8 weeks, because it had already been shipped from China. This problem does not only affect the focal company but can also have huge effects on the buyer receiving the products, and the rest of the supply chain.

The sections below named "solutions" are not ways of overcoming the challenge per sé, but ways of dealing with the challenge or standpoints regarding the challenge.

Lead-time: Solutions
The long lead-time is almost impossible to overcome. It is possible to ship the products by air, but this solution is often found too expensive. Another rather expensive solution is to increase the safety stock of the inventory. The only way to avoid the problem is to produce goods to be sold in China in China, and produce goods to be sold in Denmark in Denmark (case company A).

Costs, stock
When finding it impossible to avoid export from China to Denmark, it is necessary to invest in inventory to be able to maintain a safety stock that compensates for the risks caused by the long lead-time. This is a challenge because it becomes difficult to manage, and therefore may increase inventory costs if not managed properly. This challenge is bigger for companies producing consumer specific goods rather than standardized products.

Costs, stock: Solutions
The case companies who exported a fair share of the production back to Denmark found this to be a tolerable challenge, because it can be met with a higher degree of planning of the production schedule. The higher costs regarding safety stocks were then reduced. A way to overcome this challenge then is to have focus on inventory management to reduce the working capital and improve on forecasting abilities. Last, a possible solution to this challenge could be VMI (vendor managed inventory), whereby an external partner handles the inventory task.

R&D

As described earlier, having an R&D department in Denmark and the production facility in China decreases the level of coordination between the two, and thereby reducing flexibility. The challenge here is the coordination with the R&D department (case company H). Furthermore, it was difficult to coordinate because of Danish holidays. In China, there are significantly fewer holidays than in Denmark, making it difficult to reach the Danish departments because of the time zone difference. This subject will be discussed at greater length in the chapter concerning innovation in China, which is why it will not be treated further here.

R&D: Solutions

One way to improve the coordination between China and Denmark is to establish online communication, share outlook calendars to improve transparency concerning appointments and holidays or plan to meet at least once a month/year (case company H).

Challenge: Hidden costs

This following section will discuss the challenge of meeting hidden costs, which are defined as costs not generated within the supply chain as mentioned earlier in the theoretical section. These costs occur as a result of a changing environment, which the focal company has no control over. Therefore it is important to stay flexible and responsive so as to handle these changing circumstances most effectively and at lowest cost possible. This means having as few low fixed costs as possible. The strategy section later in this chapter further discusses the degree of planning versus incrementalism required to cope with this challenge. For the remainder of this segment, a more concrete approach is taken to illustrate the specific challenges of this perspective and how to overcome them. The content of this challenge will be divided into the topics of a classic PEST model due to the circumstantial characteristic of the challenge.

Political

The political development in China is an often-discussed topic. China is basically a communist country, but their economy is indeed liberal and market driven. But because of the strict management by the communist party, the political system is highly efficient, as they are not inhibited by prolonged democratic debates.

Infrastructure
China is a large country with many provinces that differ greatly from one another. The industry sector has in recent years placed itself on the east coast due to access to the sea (logistical). Therefore, skewedness has developed creating larger economic differences between the western and eastern parts of the country. This is mentioned in the above section about workers moving to the cities. This means that prices in the eastern parts increase more rapidly than in the west, making it more expensive for companies to be located here. The Chinese government wishes to reduce these differences and bring industry into the country by improving upon the infrastructure, which is not industrially ready in many provinces.

5 year plan and the local government
The Chinese government generates plans for five years (2011-2015) at a time concerning for instance innovation, education and growth. These plans guide the behaviour of the government and thereby the behaviour of many large companies in China, as they are owned by the government. This might be a challenge in the sense that if the 5-year plan means to reduce the focus on a business in which a Danish company operates, the Danish company can be discarded as a partner because they no longer fit into the political program (case company H). Furthermore, the local government is highly involved in the business life impacting the Danish company operating in China. The local government and the companies they own can be vital partners but also fierce competitors (case company G).

Political: Solutions
To manage the challenge of the infrastructure, it is important to follow the communist party's 5-year plans concerning improvement on the infrastructure. This location decision is vital to ensure competitive advantages and to keep transportation costs and the prices of assets like buildings low. Location in the central parts of the country might be cheap in salaries and natural materials (resources), but the transportations costs might be higher (case company A, G).

To overcome the challenges of the local government and the 5-year plan of the Chinese government, it is important to establish a positive relation with the governmental agents. It is better to be an actively involved in the political milieu than an outsider, because the local government has a great deal of influence. One way to achieve this could be to hire an external agent to manage the relationship with the government or to have an employee within the company to only manage these relations (case company C, E, F, G). Furthermore, this relation may improve your competitive advantage in that it allows you to get things done more quickly and with a better outcome. This is the concept of guoqing, which is roughly translated into "way of doing business".

Economic
Currency
The Chinese Yuan floats with the American Dollar. This makes it more expensive to export from China to the rest of the world, should the change rate to American Dollars rise. This loss of competitive advantage might be significant to some companies relying heavily on export.

Economic: Solutions
The challenge of the Chinese currency is a difficult one to meet. Trying to influence the political management of the exchange rate is a daunting task, which seems impossible. Instead, the solution might be to focus more in selling to the Chinese market, as this eliminates the uncertainty created by this challenge.

Socio cultural
Corruption
The case companies have experienced several instances of corruption since operating in China. This is a well-known challenge, which divides all companies into two categories: Those who accept this way of doing business and engage in such activities to either speed up some processes, in which time is of the essence (speed money) or where access is needed to specific resources (facilitating money), and those who reject this way of doing business (Company C). An example of this was given when the government implemented restrictions on companies to only be active during the night, where the capacity of the power plants was not fully used (in the daytime, air-conditioning took up full capacity). If a company spent some "facilitating money", the foreman of the power plant might allow you to remain active in the daytime.

Socio cultural: Solutions

To deal with the challenge of corruption is a strategic decision the company has to make and thus place itself in one of the two mentioned categories. The concept of bribery was rejected by the case companies in this study. But this may in some cases be quite costly, and a smaller company may not be able to afford this morale standpoint. The cost of bribery is often lower than the cost of losing out on a deal or access to a specific resource. One thing to keep in mind is the fact that this is common in China, and your competitor of local origin might just see it as a normal thing and a reasonable way of doing business.

Technological

Unavailability
Many of the case companies have experienced difficulty in accessing technological resources in China, because of the business they operate in (premium), which requires advanced technology. This is quite a challenge when trying to operate effectively (and efficiently) in China, because technological resources are not so readily available as in Denmark, and the production cycle time might suffer (case company C, E, F, G, H).

Internet payment
Case company A described how the now commonly used technology of payment over the internet was not yet implemented in China. This was a challenge for many of the modern companies trying to make it in China, because the companies' concept and strategy relied on internet trade.

Technological: Solutions

To overcome the challenge of technological unavailability, the case companies had to manufacture some of the technologically advanced production equipment by themselves. This was not always possible to do in China, so the equipment had to be produced in Europe or North America and then shipped to China. This was a rather costly affair, but less costly than having to develop the technology from scratch in China. Another solution was to draw on some of the connections established in China with other companies nearby (clustering). This networking was highly beneficial, as the contacts of the neighbour companies were highly useful and have low cost.

To overcome the challenge of internet payment, the suggestion from case company A was to rely on old-fashioned methods of payment. This is of course difficult for the companies who solely rely on internet trade, but a necessity to penetrate the Chinese market. A comforting development is that the implementation of the internet payment method as used by companies is in motion.

Challenge: Culture

The culture of the Chinese is a very important factor when operating in China, which is why it is given quite a lot of attention in a chapter concerning culture. The following section focuses on the challenges met by Danish companies when dealing with the Chinese culture and their experiences meeting this challenge.

Communication

The language barrier is one of significance. When offshoring, the control of the unit lies with the Danish company, and the management team is therefore often a mix of Chinese and Danish managers. This means that internal communication in management becomes a challenge, especially when neither speaks the other language. Therefore much communication is in English. However, communication with actors in the supply chain in China who do not speak English becomes increasingly challenging. This increases the risk of misinterpretation. Also, the blue-collar workers seldom speak any English at all making it difficult to train them and convey messages and task to them.

Communication: Solutions

One way of reducing the cultural challenge is to make sure that you have a better understanding of the Chinese culture by stationing leaders in China for fair amounts of time. Another possible solution to reduce the risk of misinterpretation is to hire Chinese managers who have studied in Denmark or another Western country, and thereby established an understanding of the Western culture and communication.

One child policy

The challenge of the one child policy is that the Chinese workers are brought up by both parents and grandparents as mentioned in a previous section, which means that expectations are high but also, the child is spoiled. This causes some conflicts to arise between managers and blue-collar workers. The case companies experienced difficulties with Chinese men in the production, as they were especially difficult to motivate and to keep them working (case company C, D, E, F).

One child policy: Solutions
The preferred solution to this challenge was to mainly hire women to perform tasks, which would not be more easily performed by a man, due to his physical strength. Another solution was to place the men in separate groups so as to reduce the possibility of slack. Furthermore, supervision proved useful in reducing slacking off, implementing strict working conditions resembling the conditions of the school system in China (case company C).

Face
The "face" challenge is related to the pride of the Chinese people. It is one of the most humiliating experiences for a Chinese; to lose face. This can also be a result of the one child policy, where failure is not tolerated. This fear of losing face often compels the Chinese to give a best guess when facing a task they are incapable of solving. When not monitored, the task might even not be performed, as the fear of failure is worse than the reprimand received after not having performed the task. Furthermore, the blame is often passed on to others. This challenge is again present when offshoring and not outsourcing, because the integration of Danish and Chinese culture causes conflicts to arise in this area.

Face: Solutions
To overcome the challenge of "face", the case companies explained how they respect their employees and their respective skills and guiding them at first in performing difficult tasks by themselves. Also the task difficulty is gradually increased reducing the risk of failure. This teaches independent thinking, which is a huge part of the Scandinavian leadership style.

Trust
When operating a unit in China, the challenge of gaining trust is a difficult one. The Chinese people do not immediately trust strangers. It requires both time and effort to gain the trust of a Chinese. This makes business

relations difficult to maintain if you do not continuously show that you can be trusted.

Trust: Solutions

One way of overcoming the challenge of gaining the trust of the Chinese is to establish personal relations. Several case companies experienced that maintaining the personal relationship often built trust transferable to the professional relationship increasing the quality of the relation. Also, declining an invitation to a personal event is highly frowned upon.

Suppliers

This challenge relates to the challenge of gaining trust. Establishing relations with Chinese suppliers might be difficult if one expects immediate closeness. An example of this challenge was given by a case company (case company G), where one supplier had copied the product of the case company because technical drawings was shared, which gave the supplier an opportunity to enter the market themselves. At another case company (case company D), a supplier delivered raw materials of lesser quality than agreed upon. The case companies in the empirical study believe that Chinese suppliers are more hesitant to engage in close collaboration, as they are used to cooperating in arm's length relationships, due to their culture.

Suppliers: Solutions

The case companies, giving the above examples, met this challenge by protecting their "intellectual property rights" (IPRs) by patenting their products and implemented stricter control processes regarding purchased materials and components. Also, a complaint was filed with the local government solving the issue of the copied products (case company D, G). Furthermore, establishing an arm's length relation is not necessarily a bad thing in China. It is just the way to do business at first.

Copycats

This challenge of copycats when offshoring is present when introducing your products to the Chinese market. Case company A explained that this was not necessarily a negative characteristic of the Chinese, but a part of their culture. However, it can cause the offshored unit some difficulties when their products or components are not protected by patents and IPRs are not protected. The Chinese pride themselves with the ability to reduce the complexity of Western products and thereby reduce the risk of malfunction and price.

Copycats: Solutions
A few of the case companies explained how they had allocated resources to the legal department to increase the focus on patenting and protection of their IPR's. Also, an entire department was created for this purpose alone (case company G). Another way of reducing the risk of copycats is to minimize the exposure of trade secrets (especially those related to core competencies).

Guanxi
The Chinese guanxi is roughly translated to networking or relationship management. It is a challenge in the sense that it is difficult to establish and maintain because it requires time and effort. But once established it can be particularly beneficial. The combination of trust, close collaboration and connections is powerful in China.

Guanxi: Solutions
All case companies stressed the importance of guanxi when operating in China. It is such a big part of their culture and behaviour that it cannot be ignored if one desires to be successful in China. Possible ways of establishing guanxi have been mentioned earlier: agents/employees to manage relations with the local government, personal relationship development, treat the Chinese and their culture with respect and last but not least, presence in the country is very important. Furthermore, gifts are seen as a way of showing respect and gratitude, and business cards are very important as they represent the person.

Challenge: Strategy

This section explains only the experiences made by the case companies, thus changing the setup of the section from previous sections. This is done to answer the third research question distinguished.

Deliberate - Emergent
The case study is based on large international companies that have offshored part of their business to China. Based on the empirical findings, we estimate that 70-90 percent of the strategy related to offshoring to China

is formed by the strategic planning perspective, which means that most of the strategy is in place prior to the relocation. Due to the size of the companies, a lot of planning is required, that a smaller company might not be required to. The cultural differences between Europe and China are significant so before offshoring to China companies need a high level of planning. The remaining 10-30 percent (estimate) of the strategy related to offshoring to China is formed by the strategic incrementalism perspective. Even though a large part of the strategy is planned, the study shows that not everything can be planned, because of emergent challenges they will have to be dealt with by the philosophy of "learning by doing". Companies hire agents, not only to create Guanxi, but also to handle unpredictable events to become flexible and adapt to the context. These agents are handling and acting on the emergent part of the strategy. The relative percentages are an assessment and may vary from business to business, changing the requirements for flexibility in one business. Also, the differences between the provinces in China are significant making it necessary to remain adaptive to changing circumstances in each province, changing the ratio between the deliberate and emergent part of the strategy formation.

Local – Global
Because of the differences between the Chinese provinces, it is necessary to view China as many markets and not one overall market. The local governments operate differently and the customer preferences are different, to name a few. This means that if you are not aware of these differences and respond to changes in the local context, the company's "fit" with the environment will drift and cause losses of competitive advantages in these provinces (case company A, C, E, G).

Further findings

For many years China has had a reputation of being a production hall for the rest of the world at low-cost. Now China wants to be more than that. With massive investments in development and education for the past 10-15 years, China would like to change the image from *Made in China* to *Created with China* (case company A). To achieve this new image, the focus in their 5-year plan is on innovation and education (Dalgaard, 2012) among others. If you are considering offshoring to China, it will be a good idea to obtain information about the 5-year plan for at least China, and perhaps also for the province you have in mind, to make sure your plan for offshoring fits with the Chinese plan (case company F). China is the world's largest population, and within the last 20 years, the society has changed a lot (case company E), and you are no longer speaking about how many millionaires China has but billionaires, illustrating the increase in wealth experienced in China. The distance between rich and poor is still big, and there is not a single China – but many China.

Your plan for offshoring should also make it clear, why China? Is the goal to be global or local? The case companies have moved from a global focus to a local focus with time. At the beginning it was cheaper to produce in China, and then send back the products to Denmark/Europe, but now the benefits of producing in China are minimal. Instead, gains by producing for the Chinese and Asian market can be achieved. Chinese clients are not looking for the perfect products, they are looking for products, which are good enough, and at the right price, but an increase in the demand for high quality products is showing.

The business environment in China is in comparison with other low-cost countries very structured, and offers a good infrastructure and favourable conditions for international companies. Several of the case companies were located in industrial parks created by the government, which gave the companies different kinds of opportunities. With other international companies around the corner, it is possible to create networks and to learn from each other, for instance about handling different kinds of challenges. In some areas, they had built up communities for Human Resource and Innovation (case company C), and in other areas companies received a tax advantage for settling down in the area (case company F). The government is becoming more and more liberalized, and in line with the technological development, the Chinese companies are considered more and more as competitors and not as copycats. However this is still an inherent challenge.

Before starting up in China, during the planning, it is a good idea to be in China, or at least have someone there to represent you as things will go smoother if you are present (case company A). In order to make sure that you are moving in the right direction, it is important that you find the right people to help you - people who can help you with contracts and building up networks and partnerships. Some advice was shared in order to more easily become established in China: It is a good idea to join networking organizations to build connections, it is a good idea to rent office spaces in existing companies at a lower cost in order to be present in the market place and it is also a good idea to socialize intensively in the beginning. A few organizations which might be helpful to contact are Innovation Center Denmark at the Royal Danish Consulate General and The Trade Council.

Conclusion

The purpose of this chapter was to exemplify the main challenges discovered in the literature review and challenges uncovered during the empirical case study. Then a series of solutions were discussed based on the experiences made by the case companies in the study in order to draw on them as a resource of knowledge for Danish companies to utilize. Finally, the perspective of planning versus incrementalism was discussed in order to determine to which degree it is required to prepare the strategy prior to engaging the Chinese market.

The literature review uncovered eight main challenges which were then rearranged into five main areas of challenges to be discussed. This division into five main challenges was made to divide the discussion into challenges which could be overcome by a higher degree of planning (loss of critical skills and loss of flexibility) and challenges which could be overcome by a higher degree of adaptation/incrementalism (hidden costs and culture). The last main challenge was strategy. This was included to discuss the experiences made by the case companies on the issue of deliberate versus emergent strategy formation and whether to have local or global focus.

The discussion of the five main challenges led to quite a few solutions to be used as tools to be used in specific situations.

The challenge of loss of critical skills is more significant when outsourcing than when offshoring. However, it is rare to be able to relocate an entire department without loss of tacit knowledge and quality problems. To overcome these challenges it was found helpful to transfer knowledge, implement job retention programs and bonuses to lower the job rotation ratio and retain the tacit knowledge of the workers within the company. The implantation of several 100 percent tests and routinizing of employees was proven effective when reducing the risk of errors in the production to ensure high quality products.

The challenge of flexibility was primarily concerned with lead-time, the cost of stock and R&D coordination. It has been proven difficult to remain flexible when exporting from China due to the long lead-time caused by the geographical distance. The cost of having an increased buffer in inventory to cope with this long lead-time is also a challenge, and the coordination between production and R&D becomes more challenging. A solution to this challenge is to supply the Chinese market with products from the Chinese production facility. However, if it is necessary to export, the quality of planning and forecasting should be increased, in order to reduce the inventory costs to a minimum. Regarding R&D, online communication, calendar sharing and better communication with headquarters might decrease the significance of this challenge.

The challenge of hidden costs might be the most difficult one to manage, as this is initiated in the context of the supply chain.

The political challenges include such as infrastructure, 5 year plans and the local government. To overcome the challenges of the political environment, the company should be aware of the development in the infrastructure put forth in the 5 year plans made by the Chinese government. This may provide opportunities and reduce the risk of threats being realized. Furthermore, the local government is highly influential, and good relations with these might create better possibilities for the company. It was found very useful to hire an agent or to have an employee to concentrate on managing these relations.

The economic challenges concern the currency of China which might decrease the competitive advantages due to increased prices in the export markets. Again the solution is to mainly supply the Chinese market. The socio cultural challenges concern the use of bribery and corruption. This is a moral dilemma, which each company must decide on. The concept of "speed money" and "facilitating money" can be very helpful for the company to apply, but it is mostly rejected by large international companies.

The challenge of technology regards the unavailability of technologically advanced resources in China, which may cause losses of competitive advantages for modern companies operating in China. A way to access these resources is to import the technology into China. Another solution is to develop the technology yourself or to draw on connections in China who may have the technology available. Furthermore, companies relying solely on internet trade might not be able to operate in China because of the absence of internet trade possibilities in China. Resorting to traditional sale points might be a necessity.

The cultural aspect of offshoring challenges are such as communication, one child policy, face, trust, suppliers, copycats and guanxi. The communication can be very difficult to manage due to obvious language barriers, but also because of underlying cultural differences. Bicultural locals might be the solution to facilitate the communication. The one child policy, face and trust challenges are interdependent as they originate from the culture of raising a child in China. The way of meeting this challenge is to treat the Chinese with respect, introduce them to the Scandinavian leadership style and gradually increase the task difficulty to avoid errors. The relationships with Chinese suppliers may be difficult to manage, as the culture dictates a more distant collaboration. To meet this challenge the development of personal relationships should be considered just as important as professional relationships. The challenge of copycats can be overcome by protecting the company's intellectual properties and to have focus on patent rights to see that they are not violated. A competent legal department might be a necessary thing, when operating in China. The last but maybe the most important challenge of the cultural aspect is the Chinese guanxi. This was deemed highly important by all case companies, and it is essential when dealing with the Chinese. The development of close relationships is difficult and requires time and effort. However, once established it can be highly beneficial to the company. The Chinese have a saying: *"You spend the first half of your life building guanxi and the last half of your life living off of it"*.

The strategic challenge of offshoring is to decide how much preparation is required concerning the strategy formation. Should all strategic decisions be made before offshoring, or is it better to pick it up as you go along? The case companies in this study underlined the importance of preparation. However there should be made room for changes occurring during the operation in China. Therefore a ratio was suggested between 90-10 and 70-30. The variation in the ratio indicates the diversity of China. The large country is not homogeneous, and varying preferences characterize the different provinces. This means that the strategy must be adaptable in terms of political, economic, socio cultural and technological change as well as change in the more local environment.

The last point to be made is the fact that China is not an easy market to conquer, but it is possible with determination and hard work, and the benefits of being present in the rising markets of China cannot be ignored.

One of the case companies quoted Frank Sinatra in comparing the Chinese market with the rest of the world:

"If you can make it here, you can make it anywhere" Frank Sinatra (1950).

CHAPTER 4

Innovation in China

Louise Refsing Rasmussen, Anders Ullerup-Aagaard, Anders Norlyk Iversen, Teis Bech, Rasmus Pagh Jensen and Anne Fromm-Christiansen

Abstract

The content of this chapter is based on a field study including six case companies in both Shanghai and Beijing. The empirical findings clarify which issues international companies must cope with when innovating in China. Subsequently the four types of innovation in terms of product, process, position and paradigm are defined in relation to the case companies. The chapter provides an overall knowledge of how the Chinese market structure has led to increased focus on cost innovation and how global companies should attach the Chinese mid-market in order to strengthen their own market position.

Introduction

A new global order of the economy has emerged. The last couple of decades, Chinas economy has evolved, from being a development economy to a leading industrial economy. New political reforms and liberalizing the Chinese market have made foreign investments explode, increasing the labour force and creating new market demands.

Mostly, the growing economy has its roots in industrial industries. Chinese labour wages did out-compete Western countries, leaving Chinese companies with competitive advantages in their cost structure. Production activities were outsourced, as the cuts in labour wages made increased profit margins possible. China became the world's new production hall. The massive foreign investments created a new demand for labour, meaning a new mid-market blossomed - a mid-market with a new purchase power, demanding goods of increased quality.

In Western companies there seems to be the prejudice that Chinese companies can only copy, not innovate. But can it really be true that 1-3 billion people in the world's biggest economy cannot bring innovations to market, or are we missing something? Or has these last decades as the world's production hall given Chinese companies an opportunity of organizational learning and absorbing knowledge? This chapter seeks to find out what innovation means in a Chinese context, and what can be learned in their approach to innovation management and business development.

Research questions

The purpose of this chapter is to answer following research questions:
How do international companies in China work with innovation?

1. *What impact do the market conditions have on companies' approaches to innovate in China?*
2. *What competitive advantages and disadvantages can be identified when Western companies innovate in China?*
3. *How do Western companies approach innovation in the Chinese market, and what are the future perspectives?*

Methodology

As preparation for this field study, theoretical research has been carried out to create a basic understanding of the concept of innovation. It is based on a study of scientific articles and literature supporting the empirical findings. The conducted qualitative case studies serve as the foundation of this chapter. The companies represent a broad range of industries, so that the understanding of how innovation is taking place can be seen in a broader sense. The research is based on a series of in-depth and qualitative semi-structured interviews with the Danish Innovation Center, Beijing International Studies University (BISU) as well as six international Danish companies in Shanghai and Beijing. The general procedure taken in these interviews was for the companies to have the opportunity to prepare their answers before the actual interview took place, in order for us to receive more qualified answers.

The driver has been to explore how the case companies are working with innovation in China, and therefore the empirical material has solely been representative case studies (Brymann & Bell, 2011, p. 62). As case studies have been conducted in several companies, we are talking about multiple case studies (Brymann & Bell, 2011, p. 63), which give the possibility of comparing the different cases and their issues when engaging in innovation in China. The disadvantage when using this type of case study is that statements, opinions and values are only seen from the company representative's perspective, which naturally will affect the reliability and validity (Brymann & Bell, 2011, p. 61). The qualitative analysis has been used as a part of the explorative study to identify key aspects of innovating in China, seeking to answer the research questions of this study.

The chapter contains a defining of innovation, followed by a definition of how the term "innovation" is understood throughout the chapter. Firstly, we define the segments in the Chinese market to clarify to other companies what to be attentive about if they want to enter the Chinese market. The analysis begins with a description of the Chinese market conditions, as these market conditions seem to have significant impact on how international companies innovate in China. Secondly, we give a recommendation on how to attack the market in order to become a leading player in the Chinese market. Then we give an evaluation of where the case companies are in the innovation process and where Chinese innovation is heading in the future. Finally, the reader should have gained knowledge about what innovation means in a Chinese context, and what needs to be learned to master innovation management in China.

Literature review

In the following section, the literature chosen for this chapter will be presented. The literature review will be used as a point of reference when discussing the empirical findings later in this chapter.

Definitions of the concept of innovation

The term "innovation" as a concept and perspective represents a complex variety of approaches and varies across subfields of innovation. Innovation can be seen as many different perspectives and the diversity in literature, among authors and managers, is significant when it comes to views of what innovation is. It appears that innovation means several things, and these interpretations of innovation are related to the environment and the context in which they are developed. This is a methodological challenge so this chapter will focus on the understanding of innovation as a term. The term innovation, and the characteristic of the topic, has evolved over time so the following discussion will aim to give a brief sampling and listing of the variety in definitions by some of the most recognized authors in the field of innovation. This discussion will help defining our view on innovation as a term, and will provide the frame for the further research.

Among the first authors who focus on industrial innovation was Freeman (1982). He has defined innovation as *"Industrial innovation includes the technical, design, manufacturing, management and commercial activities involved in the marketing of a new (or improved) product or first commercial use of a new (or improved) process or equipment"*.

Drucker (1985) defines innovation as:

"Innovation is the specific tool of entrepreneurs, the means by which they exploit change as an opportunity for a different business or service. It is capable of being presented as a discipline, capable of being learned, capable of being practiced".

Porter (1990) contributes with yet another slightly different definition: *"Companies achieve competitive advantage through acts of innovation. They approach innovation in the broadest sense, including both new technologies and new ways of doing things"*.

Tidd & Bessant's (2009) definition can be seen as a combination of the before mentioned *"Innovation is the process of turning opportunity into new ideas and putting these into widely used practice"*.

These widespread interpretations and definitions are underlining the on-going search for a holistic definition of innovation. In our view, we will share and use Tidd and Bessant's approach and definition of innovation for further investigation, because it is a broad definition and leave space for various forms of innovation. The broader the definition of the term innovation, the more the different aspects can be discussed. This should bring us closer to a better understanding of the nature of innovating in China. Furthermore, Tidd and Bessant's definition is well suited to describe the challenges that the companies face if they are planning to do business in China. Namely the processes of creating the right ideas and tools in relation to innovate on products or services, so that these are more aligned and well suited for the market demands in China.

Perception of Chinese market

Gadiesh et al. (2007) suggests that the Chinese market can be divided into three sub markets; The Premium, Good-enough and Low-end market. The Premium market is described as the market for high-end products for customers with significant purchase power. Premium is dominated by foreign companies that offer a superior quality for a premium price. The Good-enough market is defined as the Chinese mid-market for products of a decent quality. The good-enough label comes from customers' mentality of demanding products with a good-enough quality. Good-enough quality is making a value proposition that just covers the customer demands, but does not offer any extra features or values. The good-enough quality enables the companies to charge a price below the foreign companies' premium brands, and therefore compete in a different market segment. The Good-enough market is primarily dominated by local companies. Finally the third segment, Low-end, is defined by products of a lower quality, meeting basic needs. Products in this sub market is priced significantly below the before mentioned markets. The Low-end market is dominated by local companies (Gadiesh et al., 2007).

As foreign companies in the Premium market continuously seek to increase market share and profits, many companies at some point face the challenge of how to enter the Good-enough market. The authors suggest that the Good-enough market should not be an objective in itself, but offer some scenarios where entering the Good-enough market is a necessary strategy. The main point from the figure is that companies should only enter the Good-enough market if the state of the Premium market segment is eroding or weak (see Figure 4.1).

		State of the premium market segment	
Companies' competitive position		Strong	Weak or eroding
	Strong	Stay in Premium market	Enter Good-enough market
	Weak or eroding	Innovate and stay in Premium market	Enter Good-enough market

Figure 4.1: Market segments
Source: Gadiesh (2007, p. 85)

In cases where companies choose to enter the mid-market by using cost innovation, they can approach it in three different ways depending on the position of the company and the nature of the sector. The three approaches are: Attach from above, burrow up from below, and buy your way in. The approaches are clarified further below.

Attack from above: This is mostly companies who sell premium products. They seek to enter the mid-market by cutting manufacturing costs and simplifying their products or services. They try to broaden the distribution network while they try to maintain a reasonable quality. Before using this approach the manager has to consider how to cost innovate without diminishing the position of the premium product (Gadiesh, et al., 2007, pp. 84-85).

Burrow up from below: Many Chinese challengers use this strategy and try to outmatch under-established players by offering consumers up-quality products that cost less than premium products. An increasing number of Chinese actors move up market, which is also encouraged by increased price sensibility in the mind-set of Chinese consumers. These companies should not be underestimated as they can be the new global competitors, because these companies are fast to adapt and change behaviour depending on customer demand. Furthermore the good enough market for up market innovators can be seen as a springboard to growth and market share (Gadiesh et al., 2007, pp. 86-87).

Buy your way in: This approach is mainly used by players who cannot reduce their cost fast enough to be competitive, or by domestic players who do not have available skills, talent or technology to compete. When premium companies buy their way into the mid-market, it gives them the possibility to use a two tiered business strategy. They can still maintain the brand value of the premium product while competing on the mass market with another brand name. Additionally a buy-up, partnership or joint venture can be profitable because it provides international players with market access and knowledge they did not have before (Gadiesh et al., 2007, pp. 87-88).

Which model a company should choose is depending on their current situation and market position. However, there is no right or wrong way to enter the market, it all depends on how a company copes with the entrance challenges they face.

Chinese understanding of innovation

The definition of innovation has earlier been described from a broader point of view, but how Chinese understand and think innovation has its origin in their cultural understanding. This understanding is in some ways different from the way many Western people describe innovation. The present top-down approach from the government does not give the citizens much space for creativity or experiments. Little incentives encourage or reward the Chinese population to think differently and follow their passion for something, which is normally an approach that encourages creative and innovative thinking. According to Xu Xiaoping (2012), one of China's most prominent angel investors, this has created a population of youngsters, who are very focused on achieving the specific goals which has been set up for them such as being the best, in order to get into the right university. Students are not motivated to follow their passion but to follow expected educational patterns. Correspondently Xu Xiaoping adds that new ideas in China are not created by designers or artists but by engineers, who mostly do not have the same creative mind-set (Lim, 2012).

The midmarket in China is experiencing a rapid growth, and for companies to get a share of this marked, it mainly demands market knowledge and high competitiveness. In order to do so, companies have to deliver high technology to a low price (Williamson, 2010). The way Chinese companies do this is by using commercialized innovation where they test their ideas in the marketplace, while they are still in the phase of improving the product. To get the idea right, they might test the product 3 or 4 times, thereby they gain extremely important knowledge of consumer behaviour and needs (Dvorak et al., 2012). Correspondently this strategy also leads to a shorter time to market. Kevin Wale, President and Managing Director of GM China, states: *"The Chinese view is that it's not going to be perfect, and they're not trying to make it perfect from day one"* (Dvorak et al., 2012, p. 2). This is another and different way of thinking innovation, which distinguishes the Chinese approach from the typical Western approach.

In order to gain market share on the Chinese midmarket, companies have to be competitive on price. The midmarket is, as previously mentioned, built on the "good enough" mentality and therefore products offered to this marked should fit the market expectations regarding market-relevant features and pricing (Tse et al., 2012). Thus, Chinese companies are not focusing on how to invent new things, but more on how to change existing products so they will meet these requirements (Tse et al., 2012). How to do that is by focusing on cost innovation.

Cost innovation is one of the main ways of understanding innovation in China, and it has three main faces (Williamson, 2010):

1. Offer customers high technology at a low price. New technologies from the former higher segment are offered to the mass market.

2. The rapidly rising number of Chinese competitors offers a big variety of low cost products to the market segment that previously was considered as standardized mass-market.
3. The size of many Chinese companies gives them economy of scale advantages which allow them to offer specialty products/niche products to a significantly lower price than international competitors. The significantly lower prices make it possible to turn niche markets into volume business by stimulating a latent demand.

The importance of cost innovation is to combine existing advantages on the marked with cost innovation and thereby create a new business model, with increased focus on how to offer customers more utility for less expenditure. In order to do so it is necessary for managers to change their innovative mind-set (Williamson, 2010). By changing the business model, the manager should be keen on creating a model with focus on high technology at a low cost, instead of targeting only the first mover users who can afford paying a high price. By attacking the mass market right away, it is possible to activate latent users in emerging markets where especially value-for-money is in focus. This creates an even bigger sales platform for the company. In Figure 4.2 the traditional- and the cost innovation strategies are illustrated. Establishment of a Chinese business model can be approached from different angles depending on how a company prefers to enter the Chinese market (Williamson, 2010). For multinational companies to win market share and establish a business platform and beat domestic competitors in the Chinese midmarket mostly demands for a cost innovation approach.

However, the general pressure from the environment is simultaneously affecting the company and finally also influences companies' strategic choice.

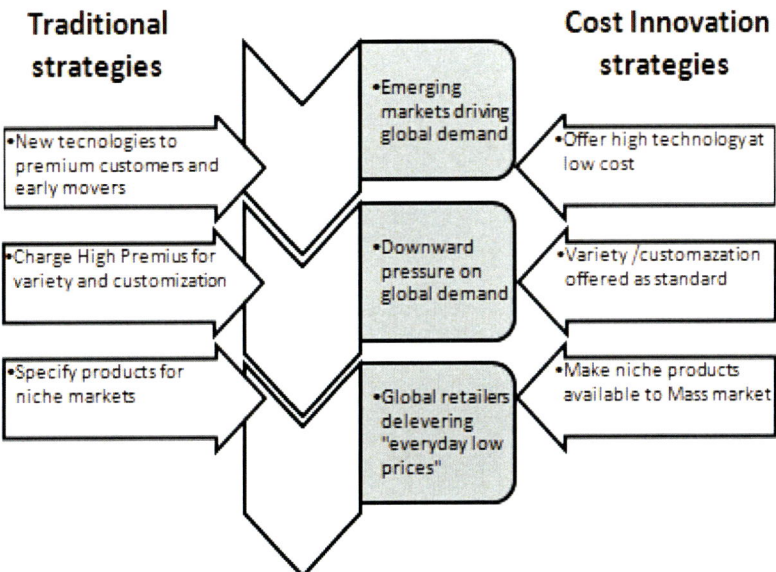

Figure 4.2: The value-for-money revolution
Source: Williamson (2010)

The term good enough is continually used about the Chinese midmarket; therefore this concept is essential for multinational companies who wish to enter the market. The good enough approach refers to reliable-enough products with a high technology at a low price. The customers do not expect the product to be perfect, but just good enough (Gadiesh et al, 2007, p. 82). The good enough market is growing much faster than the premium and low-end markets. For global competitors to stay competitive it is important to compete and be visible on this marked, otherwise they can end up being outperformed by domestic suppliers.

Additionally, the Chinese "good enough" knowledge and knowhow which international companies gain in China can be used as a hub to other emerging markets across the world (Gadiesh et al, 2007, p. 82).

Technological trajectories and dynamic capabilities

The following section is a description of the concepts of technological trajectories and dynamic capabilities, which is presented by Tidd & Bessant (2009).

Technological trajectories

Technological trajectory is a term for the strategy that determines both the implicit and explicit needs to be considered in order to innovate in China. Depending on the industry and the company's history, there will be a natural underlying strategy. When you talk about technological trajectories, 5 archetypes are defined on the basis of empirical studies, which are (Tidd & Bessant, 2009, pp. 191-193):

1. *Supplier-dominated*: Supplier-dominated characterized by all technological development is from the supply side and other production inputs and the focus is on improvement and modification in production methods. The main task for this type of innovation is to use technology from elsewhere to reinforce other competitive advantages.
2. *Scale-intensive*: Scale-intensive can be identified when innovation happens through design, construction and operation of production systems and products in order to exploit the potential economic benefits of increased scale. The main task of Scale-Intensive innovation is the incremental improvements of product and productions methods with cost reduction as the main target.
3. *Science-based*: In Science-based innovation, innovations emerge from internal R&D departments, and are deeply dependent on knowledge. The main task for this innovation strategy is to monitor and exploit advances emerging from basic research, to develop new products and/or to reconfigure the operating divisions and business units.
4. *Information sensitive*: Information sensitive is where the main purpose is to develop and run complex systems for processing information. The main task for this form of innovation strategy is the handling and developing of advanced information processing systems.
5. *Specialized suppliers*: In specialized suppliers innovation there is a great deal of focus on matching changing technologies to user needs, which also is the main task for this form of innovation.

Dynamic capabilities

Dynamic capabilities are an expression of the value-adding processes that are not to be copied by others in the industry and thereby give firms some competitive advantages. These competitive advantages are achieved through processes that are rooted in the company's high-performance routines, embedded in business processes and conditional on the company's history. Trace & Pisano (1998) have identified several factors that will help determine a company's dynamic capabilities. They are organized in three categories (Trace & Pisano, 1998, p. 297) - processes, position and path:

- *Processes* that are an expression of companies, its routines, patterns of practice and learning. Here it is essential for companies that they manage to re-configure their organizations in such a way that the organization reprocess some processes and routines that do it possible to exploit the huge market potential in China (Zeng & Williamson, 2008, p. 44). Furthermore, it is important that companies are able to embed the learning that happens in this process change, as this know-how will strengthen their competitive position, not only in the Chinese market but also in global competition.
- *Position* is the current specific endowments, such as technology and IP rights, complementary assets and their activities and relationships with customers and suppliers. As mentioned earlier, there is huge market potential in the so-called mid-market in China, but competition is fierce and it requires that companies can position themselves so they not only protect their rights through patent protection, but also exploit their capabilities in cost innovation to transform their products and turning themselves into volume businesses.
- *Path* is the strategic alternatives available to businesses and attractiveness of the possibilities that lie in the future. Zeng & Williamson arguments "if you cannot beat them, join them" (Zeng & Williamson, 2008, p. 46). If companies do not have the necessary strategic opportunities to take full advantage of cost innovation, a strategic alternative may be some form of alliance with a Chinese company that has the skills and know-how to cost innovate. There are obvious various risks associated with this alliance which the company must be aware of.

Definition of the 4P model

According to Tidd & Bessant (2009, p. 21), changes in innovation can be done by the following categories:
- *Product* innovations are changes in the products/services that the company offers.
- *Process* innovations are optimization of the working processes and the way the products are created and delivered.
- *Position* innovations are changes in the context which the product/services are introduced.
- *Paradigm* innovations are mental models which frame what the organization does.

The search behaviour in the innovation process can be categorized as either exploitation or exploration. Exploitation is the use and development of the already known and aimed to strengthen the existing routines, and can be defined as an incremental change – "doing what we do better". Exploration, on the other hand, is search of new initiatives, where the company develops and creates new routines, and can be defined as a radical change – "doing something different" (Tidd & Bessant, 2009, p. 257).

To further clarify some essential concepts within innovation it is important to distinguish between invention and innovation. Inventions are development of a new idea, where innovations are commercialization of the idea. This definition is quite similar to the definition by Tidd & Bessant, that invention must be used before it can be characterized as innovation *"Innovation is the process of turning opportunity into new ideas and putting these into widely used practice".*

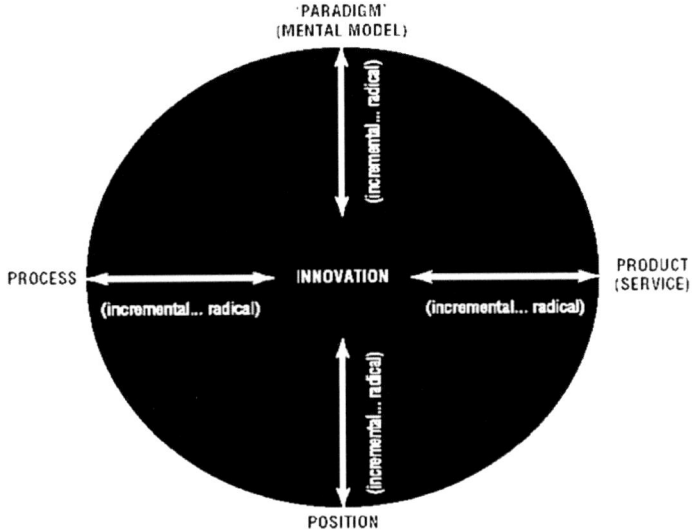

Figure 4.3: The 4Ps of innovation space.
Source: Tidd & Bessant (2009, p. 22)

The 4Ps approach can be used to explore opportunities for innovation as following:

Product innovations are designing and development of a new product or service. The changes are centred on the products and can vary from small adjustments to major changes in quality and functionalities. E.g. the company is building customized products for individual customers.

Process innovations are changes in the activity system e.g. a new production process, changes in sales procedures or internal information systems. The main characteristic is that the new process is perceived to be an improvement.

Position innovations are taking place when trying to reposition the perception of a customer's mind an already established product and service. The main forces in this form of innovations are branding and marketing activities. E.g. organizations attempt to re-frame products because of significant changes in consumer or market perception.

Paradigm innovations are changes in the perception of how a given system works, meaning what we believe is possible/impossible or right/wrong. Sometimes innovations appear, that moves the limits of this understanding, and provides us with a new mental model for perceiving our reality (Tidd & Bessant, 2009, pp. 21-23).

Analysis

This chapter will bring some insights to the table about the challenging market conditions in China, and what to be aware of as a company.

Perception of Chinese market

In the following section, the findings of the qualitative survey will be presented and later on compared to the theory presented in the literature review.

The empirical findings of the perception of the Chinese market are presented as the first part of the analysis as we suggest that the market conditions in China play a significant role in the way companies innovate in China.

The empirical findings show a common perception of the Chinese market segments by all the participating companies. All case companies believed that the Chinese market have either three or four submarkets. The three sub-markets were described similar to the premium, good-enough and low-end segments. In some cases, where four sub markets were described, the Good-enough market was divided into a higher good-enough market and a lower good-enough market. Overall it is fair to conclude that the perception is more or less alike. The Figure 4.4 below illustrates how the sub markets are perceived.

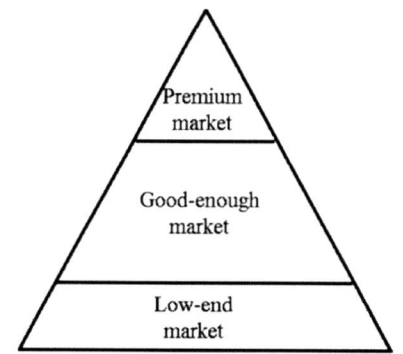

Figure 4.4: Perception of Chinese sub markets
Source: Empirical findings

Another common issue was that the companies were involved in the premium market. This point is obvious, as all the interviewed companies were foreign companies. All had entered the Chinese market with products of a better quality and a premium price. These conditions made an entry to the good enough market impossible at the starting point, without jeopardizing the position of their premium product.

As all of the companies have been doing business in China for more than a decade, new strategic issues have emerged. Several companies have experienced an increasing pressure from the local Chinese companies from the good-enough market in their premium market. This fact puts companies in the premium market under pressure, as their segment is eroding. According to Gadiesh et al. (2007, p. 85) this leaves threatened companies with only one option: Entering the mid-market. In the empirical findings, all three strategies to enter the good-enough market have been identified.

To enter the good-enough market, the authors suggest threes strategies: Attack from above, Burrow up from below, or Buy your way in (Gadiesh, et al., 2007). These three strategies are described in the literature review and will now be discussed on the basic of some of the case companies.

An example from one of the case companies (A) is that it used both the attacking from above and burrowing from below strategies. When attacking from above, the company was introducing a new brand and product. The brand was introduced to avoid any damage of brand equity of the premium brand. The product that was introduced to the good-enough market took place in well-known technology and with a lower complexity than the premium products. Quality in materials and design was also decreased. This made the company able to compete at the good-enough market, as they were able to cut costs and thereby prices. The burrow from below strategy was executed by making a joint venture with a local company. The Chinese company was delivering a brand, network and market knowledge, and the foreign company was delivering technical knowledge. New products where thereby launched at the bottom of the good-enough market.

Another case example was applying the buy your way in approach, as company F took over a Chinese competitor. This approach gave the company access to network, government officials and market share that would have required a lot of resources and time to build up themselves.

There is also an example from company C, who acknowledge the existence of the good-enough market. They just choose not to enter it, as their current segment was stable as well as their market position. Even though substantial sales opportunities existed in the good-enough market, the fear of damaging the premium brand and thereby their strong market position in the premium segment was considered to be too much of a risk.

The empirical survey has identified and confirmed the assumptions made by Gadiesh et al. (2007, p. 85), as all the applied strategies can be identified, and as the discussion about whether or not to enter the good-enough market seems to exist among the asked companies. The question that remains unanswered is if companies should enter the good-enough market for other reasons than market share and sales boosts?

Research question1: What impact has the market conditions on companies' approaches to innovate in China?

- Three major market segments – premium, good-enough and low-end
- Increasing strategic attention to the good-enough market
- If a company want to succeed at the good-enough market, use one of the three strategies – all meaning that collaboration and representation is a necessity

Integration of cost innovation in business models

Until today the world's purchase power has been lying in the hands of the consumers in developed countries. This power is about to change because living standards in emerging markets like BRIC[16] and the Next 11[17] countries are increasing. The growth is 2 to 3 times higher in emerging markets than in developed markets, therefore the potential consumers in those markets will get more influence in the future (Williamson, 2010, p. 3).

The Chinese market is one of the most rapidly growing emerging markets in the world. If a company can get a share of this marked, it gives them a good platform for future growth. However, the number of domestic suppliers in China is increasing, which leads to intensified competition among these players, but also among the international competitors who want to enter and share the market (Tse et al., 2012, pp. 1-2).

---

[16] BRIC refers to the four major emerging economies: Brazil, Russia, India and China

[17] The Next Eleven countries are Bangladesh, Egypt, Indonesia, Iran, Mexico, Nigeria, Pakistan, Philippines, Turkey, South Korea, and Vietnam. They are identified by Goldman Sachs Investment Bank to be among the world's largest economies along with the BRIC economies in the 21 century.

If international companies want to stand a chance against domestic suppliers, they have to observe the behaviour of domestic competitors and use the same competitive parameters as they do. Keywords for international companies are therefore cost innovation and relentlessness (Tse et al., 2012, p. 2). This cost revolution is a term that international competitors have to learn to cope with, because Chinese suppliers constantly find radical new ways to offer both local and global consumers more utility for less expenditure (Williamson, 2010, p. 1).

The importance of cost innovation
The Chinese consumers are becoming less willing to pay 70-100 percent more for international premium products, which is putting international brands under high pressure. The price for international brands should no longer differentiate more than 20-30 percent from domestic supplier prices, otherwise the consumers will choose local brands (Gadiesh, et al., 2007, p. 86). Correspondently to this, implementation of a cost innovation strategy in international cooperation's Chinese business model is highly important to gain success on the Chinese market. However before doing so, a company should strongly consider if it is the right time to move (change strategy) or if the current market segment is still attractive (Gadiesh, et al., 2007, p. 83).

All companies from the case studies have operated on the Chinese market for over a decade, and all of them have responded to the cost innovation strategy in one way or another. The companies all know that the future value-for-money approach will become even more important than it already is today. This awareness is important for future success. Although not all companies have adapted the strategy, they have all evaluated their current market position and used it to justify staying in the premium market or enter the mid-market also. Case company C has chosen only to serve the premium market because they believe they are among the best in their sector, therefore this company has chosen to keep their traditional strategy and only serve the premium market. Additionally, the sector structure makes the time to market longer; therefore it is possible to react on changes in the market if it should become necessary. However they are aware of the competition and pressure from the mid-market, but as long as customers are still willing to buy their products, there is no reason to enter the mid-market. The necessity of changing strategy to a cost-oriented approach if the structure of the sector will suddenly change is identified by them.

Thus, the options for the case companies to use cost innovation are highly affected by the nature of the product. It is not possible for all companies to cost innovate by compromising the product because it would be against the overall business strategy. In these cases, economies of scale or increased focus on process innovation are ways to increase competitiveness and still be able to compete on the mid-market. Nevertheless, most of the companies which have the option to cost innovate and compete at the good-enough market have done so. Various examples from our empirical study show that the companies have experienced success by taking a core product and reduced the features on this product and thereby used the cost innovation approach to simplify a product to fit the Chinese market demands.

Some of the companies from the case studies have adopted the cost innovation strategy and are trying to meet their Chinese competitors by offering high technology at a low cost. They keep targeting the premium product for the premium market to not disrupt the brand value of their core product; instead they have separate brands competing on the mid-market with focus on "good enough" quality. By doing so, they try to penetrate the market by using a two tiered strategy. Hereby it is possible to keep the brand-value of the premium product and still get a market share of the growing mid-market (Tse et al., 2012, p. 4).

How does cost innovation influence global competition

In general, multinational companies have to respond to cost innovation and how it will affect their future business. Awareness around the concept and the consequences is essential for companies competing on both the local Chinese market and the global market. The three faces of cost innovation that Williamson (2010, p. 344) describes are the ways especially Chinese companies use cost innovation to attack the market. By knowing these faces and reacting according to them, the risk of jeopardizing global companies' market position can be minimized.

Chinese cost innovation is characterized by many companies who burrow up from below. These companies do not have to protect a brand identity which gives them the opportunity to test a product in the market place before it is finalized. By using this commercialized innovation strategy it is possible to cut the development costs and actually produce goods which are fitted to the customer demand. In some cases it might harm a product, but "you win some, you lose some" (Tse et al., 2012). As previously mentioned this approach leads to shorter time to market which allows Chinese companies to react faster on specific customer demands both global and domestic.

The knowledge and know how Chinese companies gain by cost innovating, they extend to use on the global market. Local companies use the rapidly growing Chinese markets to consolidate their strategy before they go global, because if companies cannot succeed on the local market, they cannot succeed globally (Gadiesh et al., 2007, p. 82). Multinational companies should therefore compete in China, not only to gain market share, but also to defend their position on the global market (Gadiesh et al., 2007, p. 83). Failing to do so can affect future global business.

Another aspect which plays a significant part of the international market competition is the struggle to gain market share on emerging markets in general. Chinese mid-market innovators are often one step ahead because they are accustomed to act within an emerging market and therefore know how to respond to customer demand. Thus, local suppliers can penetrate other emerging markets with the same products used on their domestic market, while global actors have to modify their products (Tse et al., 2012, pp. 4-5).

Companies that react and adjust their business model to fit demand from the Chinese mid-market will be able to take this knowledge and profit from it on other emerging markets. Additionally, the developing costs can be cut radically by transferring products specially developed for the Chinese mid-market to other emerging markets. Company A and F from the case study have chosen this strategy and exported products modified specifically to the mid-market and made it a general part of their product portfolio. Thereby all parts of a global concern benefits from product innovation made in China. Innovation for the Chinese mid-market will therefore not only benefit their market share in China but also globally.

Innovative strategies in China

Tidd & Bessant (2011) describe two overarching strategies for innovation. There is a rationalist strategy where the companies base their perspective through three steps: 1) describe, understand, and analyse the environment; 2) determine a course of action in the light of the analysis, 3) carry out the determined course of action (Tidd & Bessant, 2011, p. 165). In this strategy, the companies are trying to plan their innovation through proven choices, which allows the innovation process to be a linear process with a structured plan.

In contrast to the other strategy, there is the incrementalist strategy where the process is based on a muddling through and learning approach (Tidd & Bessant, 2011, p. 168). This approach should be seen as a more dynamic and accumulative approach, where the driving forces are capturing value proposition and learning. When looking at innovation in China, there is empirical evidence that the incrementalist strategy approach is the most successful when there is a huge pressure for change on the Chinese market (Danish Innovation Centre, 2012).

No matter how you choose to penetrate the Chinese market, it is essential for Western companies that they understand how to adapt their technological trajectories and dynamic capabilities. As our empirical study has spread across various industries, no significant traces of the archetype in the technological trajectories are dominating the Chinese market. What can be said is that all case companies have developed an understanding of how important it is to focus on cost innovation - they have to beat the dragon at their own game:

"The Key to beating the Chinese dragons at their own game lies in combining cost innovation with your existing strengths as one established foreign players" (Ming & Williamson, 2007, p. 155).

In order to compete at the Chinese market, case company F has: *"(...) looked at what could be taken out of the machines to make them competitive in the Chinese market."* Many of the case companies have had to scale down their product because of two reasons: Firstly to reduce cost, and secondly there is a clear trend that added value to Western companies' products does not necessarily add value to the Chinese customers. Thus, it can be argued that the most dominant archetype used in China is scale-intensive, since scale intensives only work with adapting the functionality to its Chinese customers (Tidd & Bessant, 2011, p. 195). The reason for innovating in China is therefore not based on the development of new technology, but the use of technology and know-how to cost innovate and further to down scale corporate products to develop and strengthen their competitive advantage and market position.

It is important for companies to be able to protect their dynamic capabilities in order to differentiate themselves from Chinese competitors. The case studies have shown that a large part of the companies clearly see their way to organize themselves, with a flat and open organization structure, as one of their dynamic capabilities. This is because the organization structure cultivates creativity and thereby promotes innovation abilities (case company: A, C, E and F). There is no doubt that the Chinese still miss something in terms of achieving the same level of creativity as in Western companies (Zeng & Williamson, 2007, p. 131). This is something universities continuously are working on, which now demands for reflection and self-study, which all other things being equal promoting towards creativity.

Several case companies are also trying to get their Chinese employees to think creatively, by forcing them to take responsibility and think independently. This type of organizational thinking is largely culturally based and therefore very difficult to restructure. This gives some competitive capabilities to the Danish companies, since it is difficult to imitate for Chinese companies, due to the fundamental cultural differences.

Another part of the discussion is based on the dynamic capabilities Danish companies can learn from the Chinese culture. Among the case companies there is a strong common consensus that the capability they develop in cost innovation to compete at the Chinese market significantly strengthens their global competitiveness. CEO and area manager for case company F quote Frank Sinatra: *"if you can make it here, you can make it anywhere"* when he describes the importance of their presence in China. Another capability that case company A, which produces products of low complexity and high volume, learned from the Chinese is that they are much more forgiving. By this it is meant that through their sub brand, they have a much faster time to market. Likewise they have a greater possibility of allowing an innovation process to roll out as a high pacing exchange of launching products, leveraging feedback, redesigning, and re-launching products according to the market needs (Danish Innovation Centre, 2012).

So the necessity for all these initiatives is perhaps the most difficult adjustment of all. The company has to recognize and accept China as a source of profound complex learning which can help deliver high-tech and specialized products at a low price and at the same time improve global competitiveness. All this might be needed, as Western companies are not strong enough in the global competition, and since China is gaining more on their cost innovation approach.

Challenges faced when innovating in China

In the following section, the challenges faced by the interviewed companies will be presented. Three essential challenges have been identified: law enforcement, co-development with suppliers, and Chinese business culture, which has been recognized by several of the companies.

The first challenge is protection of IPR. The law within IPR is very clear and similar to the laws known in Western countries. The challenge to this subject is not concerned with the presence of legal rights, but has its root in poor law enforcement. As company C puts it: *"The problem of IPR is not the lack of law or legal rights, but that the authorities do not care"*. The poor law enforcement is not related to a lack of public institutions or employees, but is related to the business culture of China, where personal relations are valued more than formal rules. Another aspect of the challenge regarding IPR is that China is a country with several different regions, with their own legal system. This means that if a company has filed for a patent in one region, this patent is not valid for the rest of China. Company F explained: *"Of course IPR is important, but China is a huge country, and you cannot get a patent valid for all of China. You need to file them individually"*. This legal system makes it a costly and time consuming affair to get a patent or protection of trademarks and brands.

The second challenge is also concerned with IPR, but is rooted in another problem. Company B stated that: *"Our innovation in China is restricted to minor improvements and adaption to market conditions. We do not innovate at a level where we will need to file for a patent, as we are afraid of losing confidential information"*. Company C is dealing with some of the same issues: *"We do not cooperate with our suppliers the same way as we do in Europe, they simply cannot be trusted"*. Company F has the same perception of this challenge: *"If we co-developed products with our suppliers, they would sell our products in a month or two."* There are two problems concerned to this challenge. First, there is a lack of trust between Western companies and their Chinese suppliers. Second, the lack of co-development must be a barrier for more radical innovation, meaning both Western and Chinese companies are possibly missing opportunities of competitive advantages.

Finally, there is a challenge concerned with Chinese business culture. The cultural differences between China and Denmark are substantial and therefor tend to cause problems. That has been the case at all interviewed companies. The differences are so many, that all cannot be accounted for in this chapter. Therefore only the cultural differences, most closely related to the subject of innovation, are discussed in this chapter. At Company A the representative stated that: *"The Chinese people are not used or encouraged to think themselves. They are reliable at rules and guidelines on how to conduct their work, therefore it is a challenge to make them more creative and independent."* Another aspect of the same problem was described by company B: *"Chinese employees are not used to share their knowledge with other employees"*. Capabilities as creativity and the ability to share information are considered to be key ingredients in the recipe of innovation management (Tidd & Bessant, 2009). As the companies experience their employees to be poor at creative thinking and at sharing information, it is obvious that there are some obstacles when trying to innovate in a Chinese context.

Research question 2: What competitive advantages and disadvantages can be identified when Western companies innovate in China?

- The size of the mid-market and the opportunities for future sales makes it highly attractive, but it should only be entered if the company is ready for it.
- Chinese buyers' willingness to pay much more for international premium products is decreasing, which stimulates the global competitors' need for a cost innovative approach.
- Chinese domestic suppliers will become global competitors in the future; therefore they are a possible threat to the multinational company's global position.
- Knowledge and knowhow gain from the Chinese market can be used in the company's global portfolio. This creates an advantage compared with other international competitors, which are not using the cost innovative approach.
- Three challenges can be identified when innovating in China: Law enforcement, cooperation with suppliers, and Chinese culture.
- The Scandinavian organization's culture promotes Chinese innovation in case companies.
- Cost innovation strengthens the company's global competitiveness.
- Chinese forgiveness can be used to test the products in real life.

How are the case companies innovating in China?

Empirical data from the six case companies are gathered in Figure 4.5. The companies are listed from 1-5 where 1 is incremental and 5 is radical innovation.

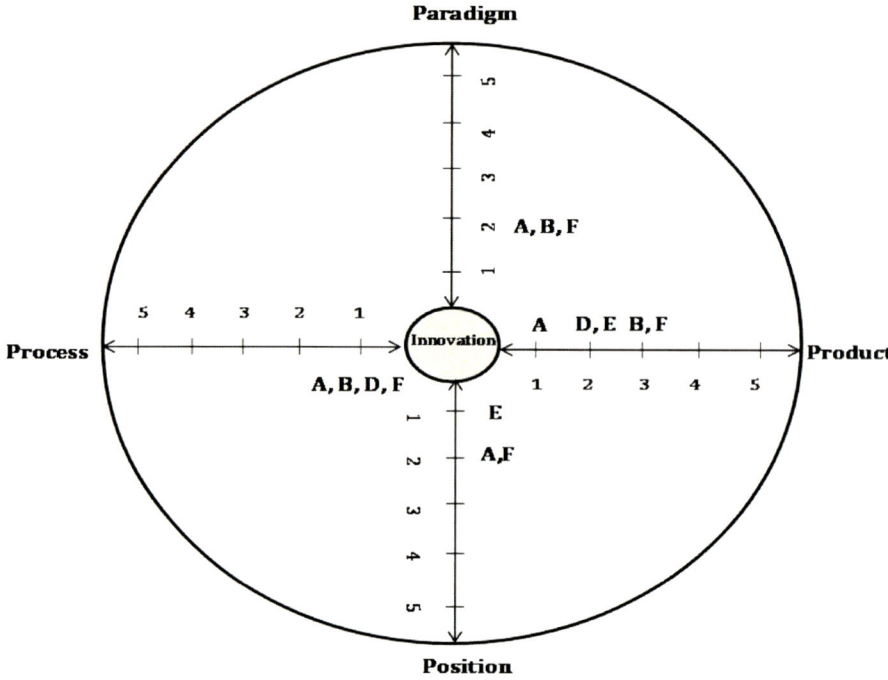

Figure 4.5: Empirical cases in relation to the 4P model.
Source: Tidd & Bessant (2010 p. 22) + authors creation.

"China has not yet experienced a true innovation revolution" (Orr & Roth, 2012, p. 10).

By this quotation Orr & Roth mean that China has not experienced a radical innovation, and as shown in Figure 4.5, the case companies in China have not either. In addition to Tidd & Bessant's model you can however see that there are different approaches to innovation, and that is also what we have experienced at this field study.

In the following chapter we describe why the companies are located as illustrated in the figure, and explain that most of the innovation is incremental changes to adapt to the Chinese marked.

A product innovation example from case company D is that they are *"adapting their product to the provinces in China, because in northern China they need heating, and in the southern the need cooling"*. Furthermore, the case companies are focusing on improving their product and making them competitive in the Chinese market *"A Chinese is focusing on other things than a Dane would do, and therefore the product is adapted to the needs of the respective country"* (Case

108

company A). And since in China there is a market where people request the same products as in others countries, but just cheaper, case company B is using *"well known knowledge in old products"*.

The innovation processes in China take place by taking features out of the product in order to make them cheaper. One case company said that *"If you want to compete in the Chinese market, you should take your best product and then cut 30 % off the cost."* As well, some of the companies are cooperating with their customers and partners to gain new knowledge and know-how, especially because some of the demands are coming from the customer himself. The Chinese partners are used in a cooperating form and not for development, because the companies are afraid that if the Chinese get too much information and knowledge, they will imitate their product if the cooperation is interrupted. Therefore the companies are cautious about IPR when working in China. Case company D takes another point of view in order to change the processes in the company: *"Every week the employees have to reflect on some ideas, and then quarterly they are gathered"*. The purpose of this procedure is that managers can see what process the employees think need to be improved.

To change their position in the market, case company A and F have acquired a Chinese firm: Case company F said that: *"we could not get into a specific market segment and therefore we were forced to acquire a Chinese firm."* Now they have gained access to other market segments and networks that was not available before. As well, company E has recently opened an innovation centre in China *"We want to get closer to the market and therefore we have opened an innovation centre in Beijing,"* This is also a way of getting the time-to-market process to speed up.

If a company has to undergo a paradigm shift, there has to be a change in the way they frame what they do in China. Cost innovation is common in China, but a different way of doing business than in Western culture. Both companies A, B and F are changing their product for the Chinese market, by making some of their products less worth than the original product. Company A: *"by taking features out of the products, we can sell the product at a lower price"*. Company B started to make light product cheaper, but since then also complicated products have been cost minimized. And company F checked their products for unnecessary elements, to make them more competitive in the Chinese market. Since the Chinese and the Western working methods are different, it can be characterized by being an incremental paradigm innovation. As exposed in Figure 4.5 no radical innovation is taking place:

"China will need time to evolve from a country of incremental innovation based on technology transfers to one where breakthrough innovation is common" (Orr & Roth, 2012, p. 10).

From made in China to made by China

China's technical and scientific capabilities are rapidly growing in the coming years. The government is playing an important and powerful role in the progress, along with multinational companies that bring new knowledge and knowhow about managing innovation to the market. The pace of change is therefore a combined progress, where multinationals will play a significant part in fulfilling the governments ambitious goals, along with local companies who increasingly and on-going develops there competences and capabilities.

China's 12th Five-Year Plan (FYP) was released in March 2011 (Stanley & Xu, 2011, p. 1). This plan focuses on building a healthy economy and growth, by developing the service sector and shifting towards a higher focus on value-added manufacturing and sustainability. The key ambition is therefore to move upstream in the value chain, by shaping the right environment for scientific development and research for the strategic emerging industries. The 12th Five-Year Plan favours innovation, and innovation has become a part of the economic targets and goals for China as it can be observed below.

Economic Targets					
Target	11th FYP (2010 target)	11th FYP Category	2010 (Actual)	12th FYP (By 2015)	12th FYP Category
R&D as % of GDP	2%	Economic Structure	1,75%	2,2%	Scientific Education
Patents per 10,000 People	N/A	N/A	1,7	3,3	Scientific Education
Population Targets					
Rate of High-School Enrolment	N/A	N/A	82,5%	87%	Scientific Education

Figure: 4.6 Key Indicators for innovation in China
Source: Casey & Koleski (2011, p. 15)

In comparison with the 11th FYP, the 12th FYP is ambitious when it comes to R&D spending activities as a percentage of the gross domestic product (GDP). As it can be observed from the key indicators, the government has not fulfilled the 11th FYP's goal of 2 percent spend on R&D of GDP in 2010. The focus on R&D spending is therefore an area where China will develop and catch up in the years to come. The targets "patent per 10,000 people" and "Rate of high school enrolment" were not a part and present in the 11th FYP, which indicates a clear sign of China's effort to become more innovative and develop their own capabilities (Stanley & Xu, 2011, p. 2).

The focus on obtaining intellectual property rights reflects the Chinese focus on creating their own products and services instead of imitating and "just" being the assembling place for multinational companies. The goal of 3.3 patents per 10,000 people in 2015 is ambitious, and will nearly double the actual rate of new approved products from 2010 at 1.7 patents per 10,000 people. This trend combined with the government's effort to provide a higher-level of education focusing on research and scientific achievements will bring the Chinese companies to a new level in the global competition, and they are fast learners. Simultaneously multinational companies will shift their roles and contribute significantly by transferring technology and capabilities that enable radical and breakthrough innovations in China.

A case example from our empirical survey has confirmed this shift, where the company just recently has established a new innovation centre in Shanghai, aiming to run the R&D functions globally as well as to serve the local Chinese market. This development will continue in the years to come and lead to a new way of understanding the meaning of value for the costumer. Value is what the customer wants to pay for, and because of that, companies need to scale up or down depending on the market in which they are targeting.

Research question 3: How do Western companies approach innovation in the Chinese market and what are the future perspectives?
- In conjunction with the analysis of how the companies in this case study the 4 P's, it becomes clear that product and process innovation are main areas for the companies.
- The companies are taking features out of the product to make it cheaper in order to serve the Chinese demand and competition.

- If you want to do business in China, you do not need to innovate much, because the basic step is to take your existing product and adjust so it fits the Chinese market. However, if you cannot get in to a market segment you have to buy your way in.
- China has not yet evolved from a county based on incremental innovations, but the innovation revolution in terms of radical innovations will be a more common phenomenon in the years to come.
- The 12th Five-Year Plan favours innovation and will bring a much higher focus on value-added manufacturing and sustainability in the years to come, which is a potential market for new Western companies.

Conclusion

The purpose of this chapter was to give a better understanding of innovation in a Chinese context. To understand this phenomenon, the following research questions were formulated:

1. *What impact has the market conditions on companies' approaches to innovate in China?*
2. *What competitive advantages and disadvantages can be identified when Western companies innovate in China?*
3. *How do Western companies approach innovation in the Chinese market, and what are the future perspectives?*

The first question addressed the question of how the Chinese market conditions influence innovation strategies by the asked companies. There exists an extreme market orientation at the Chinese market, and it is critical for companies to be able to understand and adapt to these local demands. This affects the way foreign companies innovate in China, as innovating in China is more about cost innovation, than releasing new products. The good-enough market is the main reason for this focus on cost innovation.

Secondly, competitive advantage can be gained through the increased revenues and market share which success at the good-enough market will lead to. These additional resources can be reinvested in other parts of the company, and thereby a success in China can be transferred elsewhere. Some of the companies point out that success in China is a necessity if you want to stay competitive. Another competitive advantage that can be gained from innovating in China is knowledge and organizational learning about cost innovation and cost efficiency. This knowledge can be transferred to the rest of the organization and exported to other markets, meaning increased competitiveness at these markets. The reason for success in the good-enough market is more than just revenues and market share; it is about organizational learning and development of business models.

Three challenges were identified, when conducting the survey. These were law enforcement, cooperation with suppliers, and Chinese culture. The law enforcement is a problem when filing for a patent or trying to protect a brand name or trademark. The cooperation with their suppliers can be seen as a problem, as there is a lack of trust between Western companies and their Chinese suppliers. This weakens the innovation process, and opportunities can be missed. Finally there is a challenge with the Chinese culture. Chinese employees are not used to think creatively and by themselves, which is a challenge when trying to generate something new. Also Chinese people are not used to share knowledge. This fact also challenges the innovation process.

Finally, the foreign companies in China are focused on the cost innovation strategy, when speaking of innovating in China. There has not been identified any radical innovations, as companies seek to incrementally improve by adjusting slowly. The focus has initially been on this process, and many companies are still reluctant to transfer confidential innovation projects and knowledge to China. However, the Chinese are aware of this tendency and the 12th FYP is focusing on how to make China more innovative. This will mean a shift in governmental policies and more attention to educational institutions. Given the increased focus on innovation in China, it is reasonable to assume that it is a matter of time, before we will see the first radical Chinese innovations and they will be able to compete at the global premium market.

Further research

This chapter has, from an innovative perspective, presented concrete findings and solutions to what international companies should be aware of if they intend to penetrate and operate in the Chinese market. However, the chapter does not take into account how companies must accept and cope with the reality of meeting Chinese competition in their home markets in the future. Zeng & Williamson (2007) argue that firms must not underestimate this threat, but international companies must continuously try to neutralize some of the competitive advantages Chinese companies possess. This can be done by exploring the benefits of cost innovation though introduction of new technologies and thereby differentiate the company's products through their technological capability. Furthermore Zeng & Williamson (2007) believe that Western companies must invest heavily in brand building, relationship building elements and priorities technologies. This may help to reinforce the importance of intangible assets, which increases the barriers among Chinese and international competitors and thereby delay Chinese companies in finding new ways to gain international market share. Therefore no matter if you are an established multinational, a national champion, or an entrepreneurial start-up, you need to find a way to tap into the secrets of cost innovation, because the Chinese dragons will continuously keep knocking at the door. But how this explicitly has to be done could be a highly interesting topic for future research.

The chapter also presents a theory about what kind of innovation that could be performed, in the outline of the four Ps (Tidd & Bessant, 2011). One element of this discussion could be whether cost innovation will be covered by these Ps (product, process, place, and paradigm) or whether it is justifiable that there is a gap in Tidd and Bassant's definition of forms of innovation. This gab could be where the cost innovation concept fits in. However, this discussion is omitted from this chapter for several reasons, but mainly because this would require a very extensive literature study of motivations for Tidd & Bessant's definition of the four P's, which would be contrary with this chapters purpose of coming up with concrete proposals for how international companies must accept terms of innovation in the Chinese market.

CHAPTER 5

Corporate Social Responsibility

Katrine Illum Nielsen, Maria Christensen, Jacob Wildt-Andersen, Brian Gylling Madsen, Birgitte Weinrich and Tine Husted Hansen

Abstract

The world today is strongly globalized, where trade across borders is one method to survive because of the intense competition. This globalization causes a lot of challenges, especially on the Corporate Social Responsibility (CSR) area which is a critical factor when moving a company to China as the laws and mind-set are not to be compared with Western conditions. The purpose of this chapter is to discuss the barriers and drivers associated with working with CSR in China as well as the challenges by implementing the policies and code of conduct at the suppliers to secure a responsible supply chain management. Furthermore it is to reach an understanding of how Danish companies can control their implemented CSR strategy.

Introduction

Today, Corporate Social Responsibility (CSR) is a well-known word and can be traced back to the 1950's (Parisi et al., 2009). Over the years, the concept has developed and there are many ways to understand, define and work with CSR which has become one of the buzzwords of the new millennium all over the world. One of the main reasons is the increasing globalisation which the world is witnessing today. Companies move their activities to low-wage countries or to countries where there can be a competitive advantage because of the increasing competition. When moving activities far away, they will be more difficult to control and it might affect CSR because of cultural differences. The increasing spread of the Internet and social media makes it possible for the consumers to easily follow the different activities which the international companies are engaged in globally. Also, it was easier for the international companies simply to export their problems regarding CSR away from the Western consumers. Also the media's power can easily create a media storm and damage the company's reputation and brand.

Globalization makes it difficult for various governments around the world to legislate on CSR as companies become global and move to better conditions. In search of better conditions, many companies choose to offshore or outsource all or substantial parts of their own production. A promise of lower wages and a more lenient legislation easily lures many companies to move from the West to e.g. China, but this also makes it difficult for companies to control their own value chain in full. It will quite often be a major problem for the companies, and the consequences could for example easily be that the Chinese employees work under some very miserable working conditions (Murdoch & Gould 2004), which most people do not approve off. It can damage the company's competitive advantage if they do not work with CSR, especially when moving the production to a country with a serious risk of bad working conditions. This means that there are many drivers for working with CSR, and companies are often expected to take on social responsibility. It is a clear contrast to the general approach to corporate governance in China where the primary focus is on profit rather than CSR, especially historically (Yongqiang, 2009). It is therefore important to consider how to work with CSR when moving a Danish company's production to a country like China.

It is easy for a company to have CSR policies, but they are not easy to implement in real life. Hence, it is important to remember that it is difficult to control the daily production as well as the suppliers because they might change things regardless of the code of conduct. Furthermore, it is also difficult to measure the benefits of CSR which might be the reason why some companies do not focus on CSR.

This study will answer the following questions concerning CSR:

1. *How do Western companies work with CSR in China?*
2. *Which tools can be used when working with CSR?*
3. *What drivers and barriers do Danish companies experience?*

Methodology

The approach to this chapter has, first of all, been a literature review which includes different surveys and is hereby the starting point for the questions the companies have been asked. The focus has been an exploratory research method, as the field research has made it possible to "discover" results in the companies. The purpose of the case study research is to use the empirical data received from the visited companies in order to make an original contribution to existing knowledge. Through semi-structured interviews and observations, knowledge has been gained in the purpose of making a suggestion to other companies or existing companies in China at present time. The seven companies visited are all Danish companies and will be referred to as C1, C2, C3, etc. because of anonymity. Through the case study approach it has been possible to explore the theories in the literature review, within the context of a real-life situation in the companies. (Haug, 2011)

The structure of the chapter starts with CSR definitions/CSR development and the approach to CSR followed by a description of the CSR tools. Hereafter the focus is on drivers and barriers. The last part will focus on the future of CSR, and finally recommendations will be stated in the conclusion.

Literature review

Before the trip to China a literature review was used to acquire background knowledge about CSR in China. The research has included websites, documents relevant to the research questions, and theories and models/figures from books required to high level educations.

Approaches to CSR

In relation to supply chain management, CSR has not emerged until about 15 years ago (Parisi et al., 2009). "Social Responsibility" was introduced in 1989 which included a total approach of responsibility to society.

The concept of CSR continues to become more widespread (Djursø & Neergaard, 2006), but what is it really about? It is not easy to respond to. First of all, there are several concepts very similar to CSR. There are for example "Business Ethics", "Sustainability", "Triple-bottom-line", "Corporate Governance" and "Corporate Citizenship" and "Corporate Societal Responsibility" (van Liempd, 2007). Many of the concepts above overlap each other, but they are not completely identical. In addition, there are several concepts that just sound a bit like CSR. For example, "Corporate Responsibility" (CR) and "Corporate Social Performance" (CSP) and "Corporate Political Activity" (CPA), etc. It therefore makes the overall picture of CSR very blurred. Here, however, the focus is kept on CSR. The concept of CSR is also characterized by different definitions. Different approaches to the concept of CSR can be illustrated through a continuum, as illustrated below in Figure 5.1.

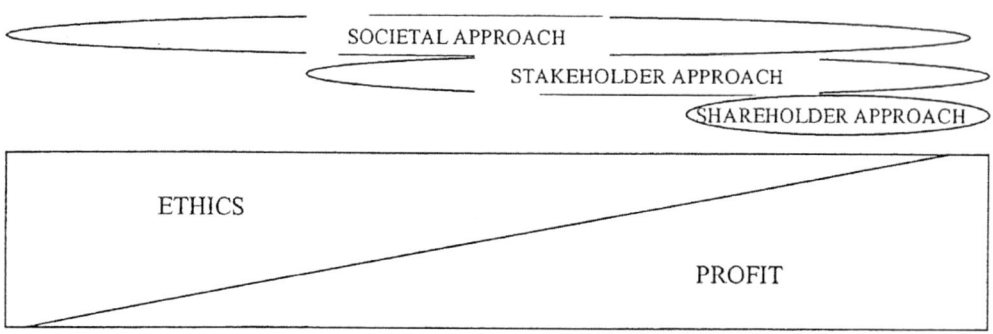

Figure 5.1: Continuum of Motives of CSR.
Source: van Liempd (2007, p. 33)

The continuum splits up the different approaches to CSR in major categories as seen above. The categories here are "The shareholder approach", "The stakeholder approach", and "The societal approach". The shareholder approach focuses primarily on profits to shareholders rather than ethics. The goal here is simply just to maximize profits. It is simultaneously the familiar economic approach to corporate governance. Here the various investments in CSR are only to be accepted if they also increase profits on the bottom line, unless the law or the shareholders request investments in CSR. Milton Friedman is one of the major proponents of the shareholder approach (Friedman, 1970). In the article "The Social Responsibility of Business is to Increase Its Profits" he explains why firms should not invest in CSR. Friedman writes it as follows:

"In a free – enterprise, private – property system, a corporate executive is an employee of the owners of the business. He has direct responsibility to his employers. That

responsibility is to conduct the business in accordance with their desires, which generally will be to make as much money as possible while conforming to the basic rules of the society, both those embodied in law and those embodied in ethical custom" (Friedman 1970).

By carrying out other interests than just to maximize profits for the company, the executive thus also abuses the money and the confidence that the shareholders have invested in the company. Do the shareholders or the stakeholders in general still want to invest in CSR they must do so with their own funds and not the company's.

The stakeholder approach takes a greater account of all the stakeholders in the company and not only the shareholders (Djursø & Neergaard, 2006). Stakeholders in the company will typically be customers, suppliers, employees and investors and authorities, etc. There is not a clear focus on profit, as other interests are at play simultaneously. Here, investments in CSR, for example, are to be accepted if customers demand it.

In the continuum there is eventually the category "The Societal approach". Within the societal approach it is not only the individual company's immediate stakeholders that the CSR activities are directed towards, but society as a whole. Hence, do the CSR activities that are being carried out by companies go beyond what the society and the stakeholders can expect from the companies? The companies simply do good deeds because they feel obliged to do so, now that they have the opportunity. This is a way in which companies is able to pay something back to the community with good deeds.

The Societal approach is backed up by Archie Carroll and the EU. Carroll defines CSR as: "The social responsibility of business encompasses the economic, legal, ethical, and discretionary expectations that society has of organizations at a given point in time" (Carroll, 1999, p. 283). The EU also defines CSR as: "The responsibility of enterprises for their impacts on society" (European Commission, 2011, p. 6).

It is clear that the definitions primarily focus on the relationship between the company and the society. The definitions above take it for granted that the companies comply with laws and agreements in all the countries which the companies operate in. Therefore, it is only the companies' philanthropic initiatives that go beyond this, which are classified as CSR.

Carroll illustrates the various dimensions OF the concept of CSR through the CSR pyramid (Figure 5.2) (Carroll, 1991).

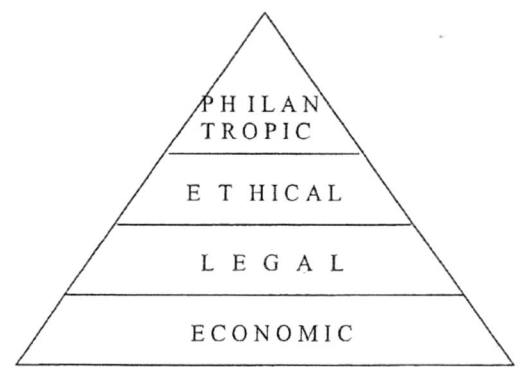

Figure 5.2: *The pyramid of Corporate Social Responsibility.*
Source: Carroll (1991)

The CSR pyramid consists of four different elements. The elements are "economic", "legal", "ethical" and "philanthropic". According to Carroll, it is mandatory for companies to meet the requirements imposed on them in the categories of "economic" and "legal". The ethical requirements for companies are not mandatory requirements. The damage to the companies can however be serious if they neglect their ethical obligations to the environment. Finally there is only the philanthropic dimension back in the CSR pyramid. It is like saying no obligation for companies to act philanthropically towards the outside world. However, it can easily turn out to be a huge benefit to the individual company to do it anyway. The company's philanthropic activities do often give goodwill among the stakeholders (Djursø & Neergaard, 2006).

To address the criticism of the CSR pyramid, Carroll and Schwartz thus constructed "The Three Domain Model of CSR" in 2003. The problem was that it was impossible to see that the different layers overlapped each other. They also meant that the top layer in the pyramid caused confusion and was unnecessary because "philanthropic" could be seen as a part of the economic or ethical category (Schwartz & Carroll, 2003). That meant that the philanthropic layer has been included in the ethical or economic dimension. Therefore, in the new model they only have three dimensions: Economic, legal, and ethical responsibility (Figure 5.3).

Figure 5.3: The Three-Domain Model.
Source: Schwartz & Carroll (2003)

The definition of CSR is thus, as seen above, far from unique. The concrete approaches to CSR will often be very different from company to company. Many companies may not be interested in investing in CSR, as it affects profits negatively. Other companies may be more positive towards CSR. This is a typical dilemma for companies working with CSR.

Drivers and barriers for CSR

In the literature, many drivers and barriers have been found regarding CSR in the supply chain. In this section, selected drivers and barriers are accounted for and will, later (in the case study chapter), be reviewed in a Chinese context.

Drivers	Barriers
Requirements from top managers	Lack of management commitment in own company
Requirements from investors	Company culture

Drivers	Barriers
Requirements from customers	Suppliers view on CSR
Organization performance	Lack of HR resources
Innovation	Lack of power in the company
Risk management (auditing)	Lack of economic resources
Ethical/moral commitment	
Positioning in society/regulation	
Market positioning	

Table 5.1: Drivers and Barriers for CSR Implementation
Source: Own compilation from Arlbjørn et al. (2010, p. 307)

Drivers for companies working with CSR

This section will describe the drivers that companies may have for working with CSR. It is these selected drivers which motivate companies to work with CSR.

Requirements from top managers
The attitude of the management, i.e. the more involved they are the better is the possibility that the employees are motivated and willing to follow the policy of the company (Arlbjørn et al., 2010, p. 307).

The culture can be seen as a driver as the literature has proven a relationship between the culture in an organization and the behaviour (Arlbjørn et al., 2008, p. 7). Culture is a word with complex cultural associations and can be defined *as the way we think around here*. Culture is also described as a set of stable and common values and methods which help a group of people to create, to learn and to share a community (Stand, 2010, p. 1). The company culture will therefore have an impact when implementing CSR because staff and top management might have different ways of doing and understanding things (Arlbjørn et al., 2010, p. 307).

Requirements from investors
The investment policy from potential investors can influence the decision-making and the organizational strategy of the top management. This can furthermore influence the CSR implementation (Parisi et al., 2009, p. 7).

Requirements from customers
An increased consumer consciousness concerning CSR will result in increased pressure on the companies in order to implement social strategies (Parisi et al., 2009, p. 7).

Organizational performance
Here it is the cooperation with suppliers and the initiatives taken by the employees. It can be discussed whether these are supporting components (Parisi et al., 2009, p. 7).

Innovation
It can also affect the innovation and development of new products which are demanded by the customers. The company may also want to have a "first mover" advantages (Parisi et al., 2009, p. 7).

Ethical/moral commitment
Another driver is the values and beliefs of managers and employees in general which will influence behaviour in the organization (Parisi et al., 2009, p. 8). Working with CSR creates a tension between social responsibility and economic profitability because social responsibility is expensive to implement which has a negative impact on the profitability (van Liempd, 2007, p. 23), see Figure 5.4.

Figure 5.4: Tension of CSR
Source: van Liempd (2007, p. 23)

Positioning in society/regulation
There are different aspects about the relations between the companies and society as a supporting component for the implementation of CSR. It is caused by the duty to observe the legal rules of society, such as social conditions, security, and legislation (Parisi et al., 2009, p. 8). Governmental regulations are significant drivers, but companies are also to respond to various stakeholder pressures (e.g. pressure groups and NGO's).

Market positioning
Finally, market positioning and demands from customers can have an important influence on organizational innovation and change. The increased worry about the "social dimension of the products" can have a direct influence on decision and implementation of CSR. Both national and foreign customers are important (Parisi et al., 2009, p. 8).

Barriers for companies working with CSR
This section will include selected barriers for CSR. These are the negative factors companies should be aware of when they are working with CSR in general.

Lack of management commitment in own company and company culture
If the management do not have a positive attitude towards implementing CSR activities, it can create a significant barrier. As mentioned earlier, the company culture is a driver but it can also be seen as a barrier. For example a barrier for CSR might be if management only focuses at the bottom line and therefore is not willing to spend much money on CSR issue because it is too expensive to implement. Furthermore, the internal coordination among departments creates some barriers, for example lack of trust between employees and top managers, working conditions, etc. (Parisi et al. 2009, p. 9).

Lack of human resources
Lack of human resources can mean lack of training, knowledge and experience about CSR (Arlbjørn et al., 2010, p. 307).

Suppliers' view on CSR
It is important that a Danish company practices responsible supply chain management when it decides to establish production in China (CSR Kompasset, 2012a). Given, there are several obstacles to meet concerning suppliers, which have a great influence and need to be neutralized before the production is properly established.

A European Survey on CSR (Arlbjørn et al., 2008) including a large number of industries, shows which challenges companies may have when trying to implement CSR. The factors in the figure have been used in the questions to the companies in China to see if the tendency is the same as in Europe.

Figure 5.5: Challenges with implementing CSR
Source: Arlbjørn et al. (2008, p. 16)

As Figure 5.5 illustrates, one of the great challenges is that CSR is not a prioritized area for suppliers in the European survey. Furthermore, a problem can be if the suppliers do not have knowledge about CSR and are not taking it seriously. An increasing number of companies are being associated with their business partners and chain of suppliers. Hence, there is a risk that the companies damage their reputation if sup-suppliers act in a way that is not acceptable for the public, especially the customers. Many companies therefore classify their suppliers in risk groups and identify the suppliers with the greatest risks as regards social and environmental conditions (Arlbjørn et al. 2010, p. 322). For this reason many companies demand that their suppliers can guarantee prober conditions at their suppliers' factories and can meet certain standards, such as international conventions[18] (Danish Commerce and Companies Agency, 2006, p. 93).

Which CSR activities to check?
The communication and cooperation about CSR is important and should not be taken for granted. The companies have to tell the suppliers what they expect in connection with CSR activities, which can be issues like:

- Human and labour rights at the suppliers

---

[18] For example UN Global compact or ILO conventions.

- Corporations with the suppliers to improve social and environmental conditions
- To work systematically with the environment and climate management
- To improve the internal employee conditions and working environment
- To develop new products or services which contain a social and environmental dimension

Lack of power
If the buyer is a small customer, in relation to the seller, it can be difficult for a company to force a supplier to follow the requirements regarding CSR, which creates a barrier for implementing CSR activities in the supply chain. Furthermore, the lack of power regarding an external stakeholder is also a barrier. As mentioned earlier the governmental regulations can be seen as a driver, but it can also be seen as a barrier, because a company may not be strong enough to influence the political regulations. This means that a company is forced to work with CSR with no political support (Parisi et al., 2009, p. 10).

Lack of economic resources
To implement CSR is expensive and requires resources. Therefore, it will not be the first priority if the company has an overstretched economy. A company can only exist as long as it can create profit, and CSR will often only be implemented if an economic gain can be expected (Parisi et al., 2009, p. 10).

Auditing and standards

This section explains how a company can measure CSR activities with the use of auditing and standards such as UN Global Compact, OECD guidelines and ILO; be aware that these are selected standards and others are to be found.

Auditing
Auditing is a quality safety system that measures the relevant quality mechanisms and assesses how the quality system can be applied to document and develop the quality of the given activities that a company wants to measure (Tidd & Bessant, 2010, pp. 595-599). This method can be

compared with risk management. The fear is that companies do not respect the social responsibility because it can cause legal proceedings. Furthermore, the literature mentions a risk concerning the shareholders when the social rules and norms are not being complied (Parisi et al., 2009, p. 7). Thus, auditing can help the companies to keep their shareholders because they can document the system/check list they are presenting to their suppliers.

Auditing will, for example, be applied at a supplier where a company would want to check or control if the principles are being followed and applied as they should be. By using auditing, the focus on achieving a more efficient and effective supplier by securing that the quality of work, health and safety, among other things, is in order and in accordance with, for example, the UN Global Compact standards implemented by the main company or the company's code of conduct .

Auditing can be used as an internal or external tool to ensure the right outcome and result of any given goal. If the company uses internal investigations, the credibility of this method will be almost useless because it is easy to manipulate with. If the company on the other hand uses external companies or agents to measure and control their suppliers in regards to, for example UN Global Compact, then the control will be much more trustworthy. It is not easy to manipulate with this method of auditing or controlling if they show up unannounced (Djursø & Neergaard, 2010, pp. 218-219).

Frameworks

As mentioned in the previous section, frameworks/standards are one matter a company can check if it is being respected at the supplier's factory. This section will outline selected frameworks/standards which the companies visited where asked if they were using.

There are many tools to use in order to make the CSR activities visible for the environment. There are many international organizations and networks that offer principles and systems which can be used in order to implement CSR in the corporate strategy (Samfundsansvar, 2012a).

CSR is often considered as being soft values, but in the past years CSR has become more tangible and organized by making certifications and regulations that companies must meet in order to qualify as social responsible. Following these principles, standards and guidelines is a good starting point for companies that want to start or further develop their work with corporate social responsibility e.g. in China (Samfundsansvar, 2012a).

UN Global Compact

The world's largest organization of corporate social responsibility is the UN Global Compact. It is an international initiative of the United Nations with the intention to involve the private sector in solving some of the major social and environmental challenges of globalization. Ten Principles were outlined in 1999 (see Table 5.2).

Area	Principle
Human Rights	Principle 1: Business should support and respect the protection of internationally proclaimed human rights; and Principle 2: Make sure that they are not complicit in human rights abuses.
Labour Standards	Principle 3: Businesses should uphold the freedom of association and the effective recognition of the right to collective bargaining; Principle 4: The elimination of all forms of forced and compulsory labour; Principle 5: The effective abolition of child labour; and Principle 6: The elimination of discrimination in respect of employment and occupation.
Environment	Principle 7: Businesses should support a precautionary approach to environmental challenges; Principle 8: Undertake initiatives to promote greater environmental responsibility; and Principle 9: Encourage the development and diffusion of environmentally friendly technologies.
Anti-Corruption	Principle 10: Businesses should work against corruption in all its forms, including extortion and bribery.

Table 5.2: UN Global Compact
Source: UN Global Compact (2012)

The UN Global Compact offers companies the opportunity for exchange of learning and experience with other companies. More than 8,700 companies and organizations are today part of the UN Global Compact. A UN Global Compact company has access to the local company network in 95 countries, and share experiences and knowledge about CSR activities (UN Global Compact, 2012).

OECD Guidelines for Multinational Enterprises
The OECD Guidelines for Multinational Enterprises, which were made in 1976, are recommendations for good business rules made by governments for multinational enterprises. It contains optional principles and standards for responsible business conduct in accordance with the laws (OECD 2008). It focuses on areas such as employment and industrial relations, human rights, environment, information disclosure, combating bribery, consumer interests, science and technology, competition, and taxation. The guidelines are designed to help companies of all sizes to act in accordance with the political and social standards in force in the countries engaged. The guidelines should help the companies with developing sustainability and social responsibility and to create a climate of trust between businesses, employees, government and society as a whole (OECD 2012).

SA 8000
SA 8000 focuses on the employees and the working environment within the company and at the suppliers. The standards are based on selected ILO Conventions and the UN Convention on Human Rights and Children's Convention.

The SA 8000 certification is for companies that meet a number of requirements in the following areas:
- Child labour
- Forced labour
- Health and safety
- Wage compensation
- Discrimination
- Work Discipline
- Freedom of association
- Right to collective bargaining
- Management of CSR process (SAI 2012)

ISO 26000

International Organization for Standardization (ISO) has developed over 16,500 international standards in many areas (Samfundsansvar 2012b). The global certifications for international standards are an on-going process. Like the other standards mentioned, ISO 26000 contains only guidelines regarding CSR, not requirements. It can be used by all sorts of organizations, in public and private sectors, and in developed and developing countries (Arlbjørn et al., 2010). The goal with the ISO 26000 standard is to provide all types of organizations to follow globally agreed standards (Samfundsansvar, 2012b).

Critical aspects of CSR

CSR is not just sheer kindness; critical aspects may also be considered and questioned. You need to be critical and investigate all the limitations and the potential of CSR activities especially in the developing countries. There are two sides of CSR initiatives; one side is the profit-making, win-win situations and the gain from stakeholders and shareholders. The other side is ignored and is aspects like power, class gender, and the poverty which can get even more affected. The tendency in developing countries is that the CSR initiatives are illustrated as being the way to solve problems, and not taking into account that it can cause more harm than good (Prieto-Carrón, et al. 2006).

This can be the case, for example, when talking about poverty and preventing child work. Children's work can have a great influence on a family because in many countries children have to work for the survival of the family. Thus, damage is made when a production is not placed in a high risk country, because the families have no place to work for their living. Therefore, CSR can be criticized for the "goodness" in some countries (Skov, 2007).

Furthermore the CSR initiatives have become a barrier to meaningful conversations about corporations according to Freeman & Liedtka (1991). They are also stating that even though companies understand their responsibilities, it does not mean that the economic and the social life are easy. It can sometimes even be an obstacle to do business that gains advantages such as cheap and quick delivery of products and good business relationships. Furthermore, the fact that CSR should be incorporated can mean that managers are involved in an area that they have no knowledge about (Freeman & Liedtka, 1991).

If a company has a CSR policy implemented, it does not mean that the financial business will be successful, as many are being forced to say they have it in the company. Therefore, some claim that CSR in reality is a PR stunt, so companies can avoid criticism, it seems like they are taken on the responsibility, but in reality are not (van Liempd, 2007, p. 30; Skov, 2007). Even though the meaning of CSR is to make life easier for the employees with reasonable working conditions etc., it also has a downside as the ethical rules can cause more damage for the individual.

A large problem which Wang & Juslin (2009) mentioned is that many believe that it is easy to transfer concepts between cultures, but they are not recommending doing so, especially not the CSR concept. Therefore, they are suggesting creating a harmony between the cultures, particularly between the Western and the Asian/Chinese culture. By creating a harmony, both the Chinese mentality and reality are taken into consideration. The harmony approach means respecting people and loving people, and hereby taking the values the country offers, seeing opportunities and not obstacles. This can be referred to the culture chapter, where the focus is relationships and guanxi, where companies have to be prepared to face the cultural differences and thus create harmony.

The case study – results from China

In this section, the findings from the Danish companies in China are being analysed in relation to the literature mentioned above. It is important to mention that not all questions have been elaborated by all companies visited, especially because of lack of knowledge in the area.

The approach to CSR in China

It was clear that the awareness of CSR was growing among the Danish international companies which were visited in China, and most of them had an actual policy concerning the subject. The visited companies explained their CSR activities with the interests of the customers and the demands they have to the company and ideological reasons.

However, it is first and foremost the customers in the Western world, who are interested in CSR, and not the customers in China (C1). The Western customers are typically used to CSR and proper conditions for the workers who produce the products, and they are therefore willing to spend extra money on CSR. This is not the situation in China. Here, it is on the other hand some different features than CSR which are valued most about products. It is the so-called "good enough" products that sell well here. There is much more about the "good enough" products in the Chapter on innovation. In the "good enough" segment, there is also a strong focus on price and therefore attention is removed from CSR. CSR will therefore mainly be important for companies which export from China to the West.

A significant number of the visited companies in China also felt that the other companies in the value chain pushed them directly or indirectly towards CSR (C5). It would typically be the large companies in the value chain, which were trying to enforce the smaller companies in the value chain to implement CSR by itself. This hereby allows the given companies to ensure the customers that the CSR activities are implemented throughout the entire value chain. If the suppliers do not meet the requirements that the customers have for them concerning CSR, they are typically disqualified and will therefore not get the order. So there is a great incentive to implement CSR among the suppliers in the value chain.

Although there were obviously some companies that worked much more with CSR than others, it was also obvious that CSR was about to evolve from an order-winner criteria to an order-qualifier criteria for international companies operating in China. So was the strong adherence to the UN Global Compact among companies. Virtually all the visited companies participated in it and many of the companies also believed that CSR activities were necessary. So it is "The stakeholder approach" and "The Societal approach", which are the dominant views on CSR among the companies visited in China. The following example highlights this; one of the companies visited in China had employed disabled people and had in addition other employees who had previously been criminals. The company was actually not required to do so in China. However, it was something that the company itself wanted to work with in China since the company had some good experiences with it in Denmark (C1).

Auditing and standards

The case study revealed that all of the visited companies were auditing their suppliers and that up to four times the suppliers were visited and controlled in regards to the standards. Visits were both announced and unannounced.

The suppliers are checked according to the standards of the UN Global Compact, OECD and ILO or companies own integrated business principles as their code of conduct. This was what they claimed they were inspecting, but as the questions became more specific, the companies showed a general lack of knowledge of the various certifications and organizations for CSR. Examples are companies which have a section of sustainability on their website, and are a member of the UN Global Compact, but the Danish division in China is not aware of what the standards include, and even takes it for granted that they have to follow certain certification, but have not been introduced correctly to them (C4, C2).

The suppliers which knew they came, question the reliability of the auditing method used. When the suppliers are visited without any knowledge in advance, they cannot make time to ensure that everything at the production site is in order. Though there was difference in the way companies checked the suppliers and how thorough they were, it seemed like it was something they had to do, but did not found it of great importance, probably because of the cost of resources.

Some companies said they took the consequence if the rules are not taken seriously, the supplier will get a limited period to get it in order.

The case study furthermore revealed that the quality of the Chinese organizations for CSR frameworks is not always at an internationally acceptable level. The companies did not have any external consultants visiting their suppliers because it was too expensive and because they did use their own auditing control every year, which they felt, was consistent with their codes of conduct. Thus, a suggestion can be to hire Chinese agencies to make sure of the quality of the frameworks so the suppliers can actually have the standards which Western companies demand (C1).

The companies expected to get different kinds of outcomes according to their CSR strategy. This was in term of a better image, marketing, positioning, and corporate governance and risk assessment. The companies were very interested in getting a more positive image and being positioned as a responsible company which is concerned about their employees working conditions. These strategic considerations were important to all of the companies visited because they had a vital effect on the company and at their share- and stakeholders.

Therefore, the companies emphasized the importance of a CSR strategy where the outcome was increased positive brand, a more positive positioning as a company who focuses on their suppliers and own employees health and safety. So the reasons to report CSR to the public and to the companies' stake- and shareholders are of importance for the company because they realize this will create a differentiated business model.

All of the companies have had trouble measuring the financial outcome of the implemented CSR strategy, but they were convinced that in the long run it is a good business model using CSR at their suppliers and in the main company as a whole. According to the continuum (Figure 5.1) of motives for CSR, different companies can choose to implement CSR in regards to the society approach, the stakeholder approach and the shareholder approach. Each of these elements is heading towards either the more ethical or profitable goal with the strategy.

Drivers and barriers for the Danish companies in China

It is not all drivers and barriers which were mentioned in China; therefore the following section contains only the drivers and barriers which CEOs and sales managers in the companies have given their extensive knowledge about.

Drivers in China
Requirements from top managers and ethical behaviour
The companies' approach is depending of this. However, the organizational culture is important everywhere because there is a considerable difference in the culture in China compared to Denmark.

Danish companies therefore need to consider whether they want to practise Danish or Chinese leadership (C2). A major difference is the management style, which is more authoritarian in China than in Denmark.

It has been shown that there is a clear link between organizational culture and employee behaviour. It can be a driver for the company to have a culture that appreciates gender, and is aware of the work and living conditions for employees. Finally, the leaders of the visited companies believe that the decisive factor is that they support 100% their staff and their projects and hereby show social responsibility (C5). Furthermore, the leaders are trying to be role models for the employees by showing them that it is not allowed to "steal" from the company, such as soap and toilet paper, because they are not doing it themselves. There was also an example with office supplies, where the employees got new supplies before the managers, simply to show them that they have great importance for the company (C4, C5).

All the respondents had ethical drivers for CSR because they consider CSR as the *"right way to do things"* but how this driver was expressed was not done in the same way in all companies. Managers have their individual values which affect how CSR is used in a company. Some managers used their own behaviour to set an example for their employees which reflected the Western style of leadership. This was done in order to show the employees the *"right way to do things"*. The case study showed that not all managers had the same level of ethical drivers regarding CSR. This means that even though better working conditions are in focus, the managers are still aware of the need to control employees' demands (C1). This created a tension between social responsibility and economic profitability which was described in the literature.

Requirements from customers
To be aware of their CSR policies is an advantage for companies. This is reflected by the fact that more of their customers in the West are becoming more aware of social responsibility. This is because customers want to do business with companies that they know have a good brand and do not use child labour in the productions. Until now it is primarily the customers in the Western world who focus on CSR, while the interest from the Chinese customers is weak.

Organizational performance
The companies all stated that they were working out contracts with the suppliers to elaborate which demands they have concerning CSR. Here, is it important to have the "good" relationship with the suppliers and the collaborators. Thus, the focus on guanxi (as the culture chapter mentions) is one source to good organizational performance and created greater value for the company (C4, C6).

Barriers in China
Company Culture
As mentioned, the culture can be defined *as "the way we think around here"*, which can be diffucilt to change.

"Implementing CSR in China cannot be done from one day to another. It will take time because the culture and values have to be changed" (C5). Another company also

had this opinion and said that it is a radical change when you implement a CSR strategy, because you have to change their mind-set and culture, which is something you cannot do from one day to another. It is necessary to tell them what is going to happen or else no-one is able to follow (C6).

In China, Chinese top managers often do not care about the working conditions, and many employees are more focused on their salary than on their working conditions. However, the managers do not want the employees to work more hours than the law allows, but the employees might want to because of overtime. It is necessary for the managers to explain why the employees should not work so many hours if they are to comply with the regulations the government has made (C1, C5, C2).

The case study also revealed that employees are willing to quit their job for a better salary or for more hours even thought this means worse working conditions. They are also willing to go on strike because of the payment (C2). To improve the working condition one of the companies has regular employee satisfaction surveys and conversations (C7).

Suppliers' view on CSR
According to the case study in China, CSR is important for Western companies, but is beginning to become a priority in Chinese companies as well. This is necessary because the companies cannot sell their products if the regulations are not being kept, it will especially be a problem to sell to Western companies. However, it is still difficult to do business with the Chinese companies and the Chinese suppliers because they are not obligated to follow any rules or principles as the Western countries are (C7).

"You cannot educate Chinese in CSR. It is a matter of China becoming a global player; they have to follow the others in the field" (C6). This quote from a CEO points out that the Chinese do not have the knowledge about CSR, but have to open their eyes for what is important if they want to deliver to Danish as well as other global companies in China. As mentioned earlier, is it not possible to change a mind-set or a culture from one day to another. Therefore, the understanding of where they are coming from and what they are thinking and understanding about CSR is important, before helping them with this change (C6).

The main challenges which the Danish companies are facing with their suppliers are (C1, C3, C4, C6, C7):

- Supplier knowledge and understanding: The suppliers in general know what is right or wrong, but the problem is that proper conditions cost money so they have trouble taking it seriously. Problems at the suppliers are often:
    o Working conditions: The firms must take care of production planning in a safe and healthy way.
    o Working time and rest: The firms must take care of work limitation, i.e. that the employees do not work more than permitted per week and that they get the legitimate rest. In China minimum 3 pauses per day and lunch paid.
    o Child labour: For example minimum age, work type, work hours, wages and work environment. It is important for all the firms visited to avoid this.
    o Discrimination: All employees in the organization and with their suppliers must have equal rights regardless of gender, race, religion, etc.

These bullet points can be seen in contrast to the above mentioned activities to check, when visiting suppliers. Some of the Danish companies are already helping their suppliers with practicing CSR by training them and showing them their code of conduct. The biggest challenge is to make them understand the importance of this training, which was the third factor in Figure 5.5. As a logical consequence if the suppliers do not meet the expectations, they cannot continue the corporation with the company (C1, C4, C6).

It can, at some point, be difficult because the supplier is so unique that it would be a disaster to break away from the corporation (C3). The advantage with this training of suppliers is that the companies can get ahead of the regulations and are ready for changes. Hence, if the headquarter makes new rules, then the change and acceptance at the supplier side will be easier because of the training (C1).

Furthermore, it strengthens the companies' image and reputation when they are showing their CSR policies to the surrounding world, but that is mostly for Western customers as many Chinese suppliers do not have the knowledge and priority of CSR, as mentioned above (C1, C3).

The companies were asked several questions about the social and environmental conditions and they seemed like they found it important, but the fact that they had to think about it and hesitated to answer gives doubt to the answers. At some point the answers seemed like something they *had* to say, but did not mean. Furthermore, at some of the factories the employees in the productions did not wear masks, gloves or other protection equipment. Thus, one conclusion can be that the managers are saying that they are following the rules of proper working conditions, set by the Danish headquarter in Denmark, but by observations the opposite is shown. If the companies do not have the conditions in order in their own plant, then it is hard to demand suppliers to follow their rules.

Lack of human resources (Knowledge and experience)
According to the Danish companies in China, the knowledge and experince with CSR is very limited. The Chinese do not know much about this subject and education can therefore be necessary. This was especially seen in one of the companies which have to go through a learning process (C5). They had spent one and a half years to implement their CSR strategy. In other words this is an issue which takes time and will be in constant development.

The manager here uses himself as a role model on how to behave, which has had a positive effect, and the Chinese staff approves the Western leadership style. There were several companies that used e-learning and tests to educate their manager in CSR.

Lack of power in own company
The case study has shown that the cultural difference between China and Denmark makes it difficult to introduce CSR because the values are not the same (C5). It is difficult to enforce the Danish CSR strategies, especially to the supplier, because there is not enough legislation protecting (C1, C2, C5, C6).

This statement can be confirmed by a country profile of China. This profile shows that there is not enough legislation protecting the workers, and forced labour and holding the workers' salary happens quite often. However, one of the companies said that there is an increasing focus on CSR from the government (C5).

Economic resources
It was mentioned that it is difficult to measure the economic results and it is difficult to know how much money the company should invest in CSR (C1). However, they do not compete under the same conditions as Chinese

competitors, which gives them a competitive advantage because they do not spend extra money on better working condition (C7).

The future of CSR in China

Through the observations in China it is clear that the importance of CSR has increased during the past years. Suppliers have also been an important part of a company's value chain, and the relations to the suppliers have been given more attention in regards to sustainability programs. This is true not only for the individual company, but for the entire value chain the company operates in. The visit in China showed that CSR has become more important in recent years and companies are implementing a CSR strategy to a higher degree, but there is still a long way to go. But as the case study showed, is it the Western companies that should act like role models and set up the rules for the future when it comes to CSR. The Chinese customers do not have as much money as the customers in general have in the West. Therefore, if CSR should become a common language in China, it requires that the Chinese customers earn more money. If they are able to afford more expensive products, then they are willing to buy the product with the value added aspect such as CSR.

Corporate Social Responsibility cannot be ignored especially among the suppliers. They will thus not come into consideration among the Western companies if they will not work with CSR, because the customers in the West demand that the companies have the complete control over their supply chain or else they will not buy. It can therefore be expected that CSR will continue to spread among enterprises in China if they are to sell and cooperate with the West.

Eventually, a need will arise in the future to develop methods to control the financial outcome of a company's CSR strategy, because if the companies can see improvement in their economy, then the possibility for the Chinese companies to implement a CSR strategy will increase.

Where to seek help?

Danish companies can seek help from different places in China if there is doubt about the suppliers they have found. One possibility is to contact the Danish embassy in Beijing which can help setting the ground rules for the suppliers (Albertsen, 2011). It is also possible to contact the local consulate which has Chinese employees and consultants who inspect the companies.

The locals often know what to look for under the surface in the companies, which foreigners do not (Christensen, 2011).

Another help foreigners can seek in order to succeed concerning responsible supplier management is the CSR compass (www.csrkompasset.dk). This tool was developed in 2005 and is a guide to effective supply chain management. The website has cases and small video clips which include practical know-how about CSR. Furthermore, *Rådet for Samfundsansvar* (www.raadetforsamfundsansvar.dk) can help as they have drawn up a line of directions about how companies can create better social and environmental relationships with suppliers (CSR Kompasset, 2012).

Conclusion

The CSR approach depends on to whom and why a company want to position itself. If a company produces to the Chinese market, then the shareholder approach is in focus because the Chinese is satisfied with the good-enough-products. On the other hand, companies who produce to Western customers have the societal approach or the stakeholder approach because Western customers demand CSR at the producers' factory as well as the suppliers.

The tools used it China were primarily auditing to check if the suppliers where using the correct standards/tools such as UN Global, ILO or OECD, or the company's own code of conduct which the suppliers had been presented to. But a problem occurred when asking the companies about the standards. They claimed that they were checking if the suppliers were keeping them, but how they could do that without having own prober knowledge about them, takes a leap in the dark! Therefore, it can mainly be seen as a buzzword that companies just need to say to satisfy others; sadly this was the tendency among some of the Danish companies. However, this statement does not mean that all Danish companies in China lack knowledge about CSR.

Several drivers and barriers were found in the literature review, but not all of them were found in China. One of the main drivers is an increasing demand from the customers. This is especially the case for the Western customers, because CSR still is not so important for companies who only produce products to the Chinese market, because the Chinese customers are satisfied with the good-enough-products as mentioned above. Furthermore, if the individual companies are unable to meet the different requirements for CSR from the customers, the consequence is often that the company does not get the order. Thus, there is a strong incentive to implement CSR for the companies who export their products from China and back to the West. It is clear that CSR is evolving from an order-winner criterion to an order-qualifier criterion in China. This is the case for companies who work closely with companies in the West or companies who export directly to the West.

The cultural differences were also a main barrier, where it became clear that the Chinese employees only focused on earning money and not on their own safety. Thus, is it difficult to convince them that CSR is an important matter. Furthermore, the language and the mind-set is a barrier which is difficult to overcome and clearly is a fact new companies should have in mind before entering China. Many questions can still be unsolved for companies so those who want to try to be successful in China can seek help at the Danish embassy in Beijing. Furthermore, several websites can be used such as: csrkompasset.dk and raadetforsamfundsansvar.dk.

As a final remark you have to be aware that you should be careful to "copy" something ethical or something ideological to China because there are other procedures to be used. You have to take the cultural differences into account and create one harmony instead of forcing a concept down upon a different culture than your own.

CHAPTER 6

Epilogue: Learning and Reflection

Ole Stegmann Mikkelsen and Jan Stentoft Arlbjørn

Abstract

This chapter summarises and concludes on the process, the results, and the technical as well as social learning elements for the students participating. The chapter is based on the students' answers to an evaluating questionnaire survey. The chapter ends with extracting the overall conclusions for the four themes of the field study trip.

Introduction

This chapter is a reflection on the course *International Field Studies* offered by the Department of Entrepreneurship and Relationship Management at the University of Southern Denmark in Kolding. In the course description, the objective of the course is stated as:

> *'The aim of International Field Studies is to develop the students' skills in applying specific theories and approaches from a general ontological, epistemological, and methodological perspective to a concrete business problem in a problem driven collaboration with other students. Furthermore, the purpose is also for the students to obtain experience with the necessary technical, social, and ethical competencies required in conducting international field work.'*

Thus, the aim of the course is to develop the students' skills in conducting all phases of a smaller field study, including the preparatory desk research, the organization of the field work, and the completion of subsequent analyses and reports.

In order to follow up on the purpose of the course, the students were asked to fill in a brief online questionnaire shortly after returning to home from China. The questionnaire included eight questions of which three were open ended allowing the students to reflect and comment on their experience and learning. The rest of the questions were answered on a 7-point Likert scale (1 = low degree of agreement and 7 = high degree). Of 22 enrolled students, 20 students answered the eight questions. The results of this survey are presented here as it is believed they can provide learning to others outside the department in which the course is offered. For example the results may be of interest to other persons in the process of planning or executing a similar course. Furthermore, as the composition of the course puts the students in physical proximity to the core content of the theoretical studies, it can contribute to the continuous discussions on creating stimulating learning environments, also in courses of longer duration.

The chapter is further on organized in short sections in which the students' feedback is presented on the most impressive experiences during the field study trip. The chapter ends by presenting conclusions on the overall study trip and brief conclusions on the respective student chapters' findings.

Most impressive experiences

The students were asked to reflect on and rank what had been the three most impressive experiences during the field study trip. The results are:

1. First-hand experience the difference between Danish and Chinese culture
2. The company visits, which also gave better business understanding
3. The social aspect of being together as a group

The students were likewise asked to evaluate whether the course gave them a better understanding of relevant theories to be used to solve their research questions. The results of this question are shown in Figure 6.1.

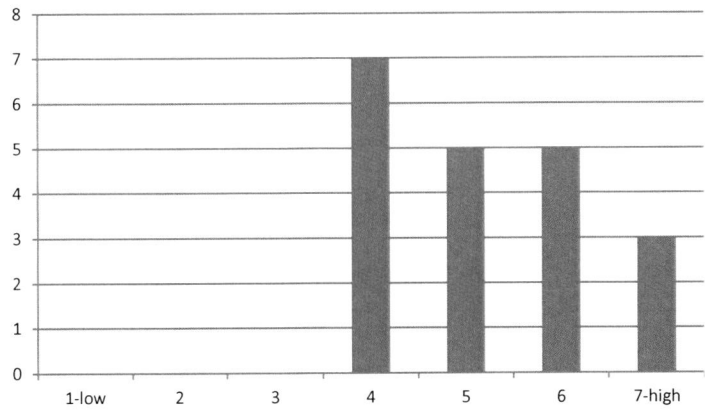

Figure 6.1: Better Understanding of Relevant Theories and Methods

With an average score of 5.20, on a seven point scale, and the distribution illustrated in Figure 6.1, it can be concluded that the students find that they have obtained a better understanding of relevant theories and methods during the course. The close presence with the subject matter in China has provided the students with new understandings of theories and methods taught in Denmark, and how to adjust these to other contexts. Thus, students should not only learn the relevant theories, but they should also understand their limitations and how to apply them in practice.

Application of relevant theories and methods

The students were also asked to evaluate the degree to which they were challenged in using relevant theories and methods in order to solve their research questions stated in their respective assignments. The result is illustrated in Figure 6.2.

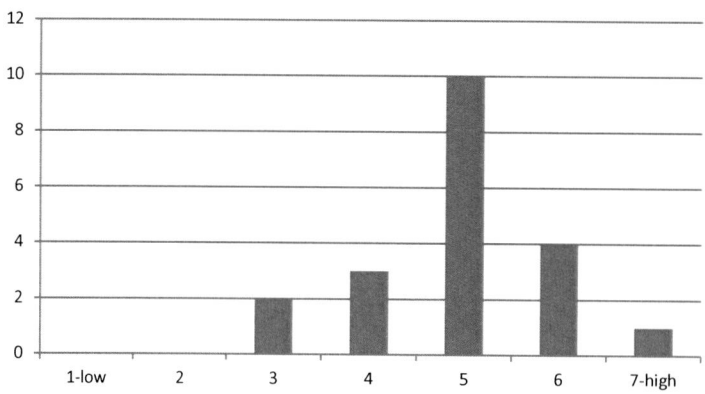

Figure 6.2: Application of Relevant Theories and Methods

The result of this question indicates that the students feel they have been somewhat challenged by finding theories to be used in order to cover their research questions stated in their assignments (see chapter 2 to 4). The average is 4.95 on a seven point scale. A general observation is that the groups, before the field study trip, found themselves relatively confident with their theory selection. However, their stay in China with the interviews, observations and personal presence in the Chinese culture gave them a more nuanced view of theories and methods and how to apply them.

Improved competencies through group work

The students were then asked to evaluate to which degree participation in the course had improved their competencies (in conducting group work). Results to this question are shown in Figure 6.3.

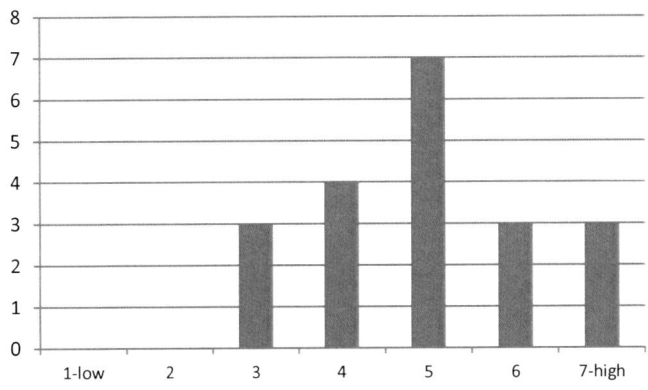

Figure 6.3: Improved Social Competencies through Group Work

Looking at the answers, it seems that most of the students perceive that they have improved their social competencies with respect to group work from a medium to a high degree. The average score on this question is 4.95. At the time of the evaluation, the students were back in Denmark and still in the process of writing up their assignments. Up to this point, they have mainly been working with the theories and methodologies for their assignment, and data analysis had just begun. Not all four groups organized the work in the same way. Some groups worked together in all aspects of the assignment, while others divided the group into sub-groups with specific responsibilities.

Better understanding of Chinese culture

The students were additionally asked to reflect upon whether the field study trip has provided them with a better understanding of Chinese culture. The results are illustrated in Figure 6.4.

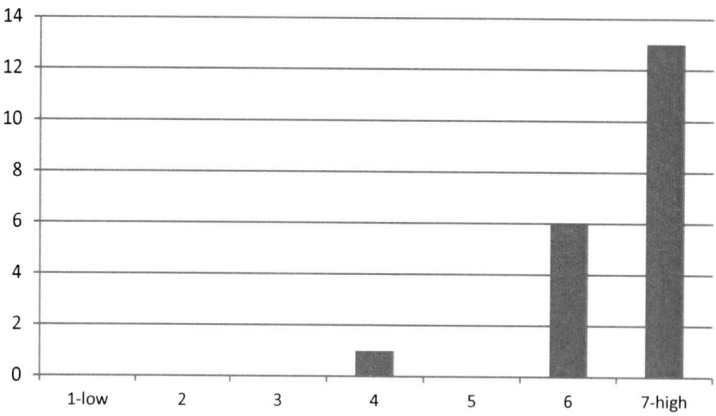

Figure 6.4: Better Understanding of the Chinese Culture

Given the results in Figure 6.4, there is a significant indication that the field study trip has provided the students with a better and deeper insight into Chinese culture and society. The average score on this question is 6.55. The overall program was comprehensive with company visits. The visited companies excelled in including cultural aspects of doing business in China in their presentations and discussions. This provided the students with first and second hand insights from people actually living in the culture. Together with actually being in Chinese cities, this has given them much cultural learning and understanding.

The most important points of cultural learning

The students were asked what they perceived as the most giving cultural learning from the field study trip. The question was open ended and the elements most often mentioned are summarized below.

- The speed of change in China
- Communication: "yes" is not always a "yes"
- China is not one country - provinces must be treated as different markets
- The importance of Guanxi (relationship management)
- Money talks
- Speed in execution of decisions

- The significance of cultural understanding and market adaption to survive in business

Conclusion

This book is entitled "Doing Business in China: Report from a Field Study Trip". The global economy is becoming more complex through global sourcing and trade from all over the world. The themes for the students have been chosen due to their practical relevance for the present time. Due to increased business activity with Chinese companies, the concept of *Chinese business culture* is important to study. In the West, many companies have discussed China on board meetings, both in terms of China as low cost sourcing, as a low-wage production destination and more lately in terms of China, with its high population, as an emerging market for selling products. Therefore, *offshoring* has been considered as an important theme to investigate during the field study trip. From a manufacturing perspective, China has for many years been perceived as the low skilled "arm's and leg's" production site of the world. However, China is rapidly transforming itself from a low cost country to a high value country in terms of innovative products. Therefore *innovation in China* as a theme was included. Given the globalization in trade and production, *Corporate Social Responsibility* (CSR) is an issue that has been lifted into the board rooms and has become a strategic element in many companies. Companies will be held responsible for the behaviour in their supply chain on issues such as the use of child labour and employee working conditions. Therefore, it was a natural choice to also investigate how the visited companies have dealt with the challenges of CSR when doing business in China.

Conclusions on the questions of each of the four themes are briefly provided in the following.

Chinese business culture

In the chapter on Chinese business culture, the following questions guided the research:

- What is the foundation of Chinese business culture?
- What is essential for Danish companies to be aware of when entering China?

- What is the potential for Danish companies in China concerning future business?

Chinese behaviour is a mix of old Chinese traditions and the economic and political changes experienced in the last century, and not least the last decades. Guoqing and Guanxi are important concepts to understand. Closely related to Guanxi are trust and the concept of not losing face. These are essential aspects to understand and master when manoeuvring in the context of Chinese business culture. In a Western context, exchange and transactions are most important and relationships follow, while in a Chinese context relationships are more important. To create network and personal relationships it is important not to lose face on either side. Managers are still requested to supervise the Chinese workers more than in Denmark and to make more detailed work instructions to get things done. However, this is changing. China still struggles with work environmental issues as well as corruption, and this is on the agenda for the newly elected Chinese government.

Offshoring to China, drivers and barriers

The aim of this chapter was to investigate and exemplify the main challenges of offshoring to China and to understand the learning. The chapter sets out to answer the following questions:

- What are the challenges of operating in China?
- How can one meet the challenges of operating in China?
- Should a company plan everything before offshoring or learn as they go along?

Based on a literature review and discussion with the visited companies, four groups of challenges when operating in China, were identified: loss of critical skills, flexibility, hidden cost and culture. A fifth challenge added is strategy as the degree to which preparation can be made prior to the offshoring process is an important aspect of the chapter. Loss of critical skills is found to be rooted in the challenges of tacit knowledge due to high blue collar job rotation and replacing Danish white collars with Chinese white collars. Flexibility challenges are cantered on lead-time, inventory build-up and the (physical, mental and time) distance between R&D located in Denmark and manufacturing located in China. Hidden costs are the cost rooted in Chinese political decisions (e.g. focus on west China raises labour cost in east China), currency, socio cultural (corruption) and unavailability of technology. Yet another challenge is culture. Not only is communication challenging, but companies need to understand the difference and importance of trust, of not losing face and Guangxi (relationship). Also the issue of copycats is a cultural challenge to focus on when offshoring to China. The final challenge is concerning if a company should plan all before or learn as they go along. The visited companies had a planning perspective up front with most of the strategy in place before the relocation. However, the companies found that not all can be planned, why some of the strategy related to the offshoring is formed by a strategic incrementalism perspective.

A further finding was that the focus for being in China has changed. In the beginning, China was chosen due to its low labour cost, while the location in China is now due to the needed market presence in a booming Asian/Chinese market. In this light, it is important to understand that China is not one market, but is constituted by several markets. Customer preferences are different, and local government operates differently in the various provinces.

Innovation in China

The chapter on innovation provides an overall knowledge of how Chinese market structure has led to increased focus on cost innovation, and provides an increased understanding of innovation in a Chinese context. To understand this phenomenon, the following research questions were formulated:

- What impact has the market conditions on companies' approaches to innovate in China?
- What competitive advantages and disadvantages can Western companies benefit to innovate in China?
- How do Western companies approach innovation in the Chinese market and what are the future perspectives?

The change in the "why" of being in China from using China as a low cost manufacturing location, to being in China to be close to the market affects the way innovation is perceived in the companies visited. The significant presence of the harsh competition in the mid-market effects the way foreign companies innovate in China, as innovating in China is more about cost innovation, than releasing new products. This poses new challenges on the companies in terms of innovation. The shorter time to market (TTM) and the speed in feedback from the market and changes in market preferences increase the demands on the companies. At the same time, the Chinese government in their newest five year plan emphasize the focus on China as an innovative country stressing the ambition from "Made in China" to "Made by China".

Corporate Social Responsibility

With the globalization of trade, having a strong focus on CSR has become even more important. This also applies to a Chinese context. A company entering China needs to gain an understanding of the CSR issues related to the national context. In the chapter on CSR, three main questions were formulated to lead the search for practice in a Chinese context:

- How do Western companies work with CSR in China?
- Which tool can be used when working with CSR
- What drivers and barriers do Danish companies experience

Through the discussions it became clear that the awareness of CSR is growing among the Danish companies visited.

The findings suggest that there are several issues that a company must take into account when doing business in China. The Danish companies rely on auditing the supply base on their compliance to company CSR code of conducts. The codes of conducts are based on standards such as UN Global Compact, ILO or OECD. The companies expressed several drivers and barriers to implementing CSR. A main driver is the increasing demand from especially Western customers, but also due to ideological reasons. When dealing with CSR in China, it is important to understand that China is a very different country compared to Western countries. The Chinese customers do not yet demand the same level of CSR compliance as Western companies. However, this might change as Chinese companies expand their operations to target Western consumers. A positive aspect is that companies use CSR to recruit and retain qualified employees.

All the visited companies have formulated CSR policies. However, it seems to be challenging to enforce corporate CSR policies to a full extend in a Chinese context. This is not only due to Chinese culture and the Chinese suppliers view on CSR. In most companies a gap between the "talk and the walk" was experienced. As with many other corporate initiatives – the more distant from the corporate centre, the harder it is to implement and enforce.

References

Albertsen, S. (2011): Skik følge eller deal fly – få hjælp hos ambassader og konsulater, available at: http://www.youtube.com/watch?v=7sWR_1sLC3M&feature=youtu.be , accessed 30th November 2012.

Arlbjørn, J.S., Lüthje, T., Mikkelsen, O.S., Schlichter, J. & Thoms, L. (2013) *Danske producenters udflytning og hjemtagning af produktion*, Kraks Fond Byforskning, København K.

Arlbjørn, J.S. & Lüthje, T. (2012), "Global operations and their interaction with supply chain performance", *Industrial Management & Data Systems*, Vol. 112, No. 7, pp. 1044-1064.

Arlbjørn, J.S., de Hass, H. Mikkelsen, O.S., & Zachariassen, F. (2010): *Supply Chain Management: Sources for Competitive Advantages*. Academica, Aarhus.

Arlbjørn, J.S., Rasmussen, B.W., Liempd, D. & Mikkelsen, O.S. (2008): *A European Survey on Corporate Social Responsibility*, Institute for Entrepreneur and relationship management, University of Southern Denmark, Kolding.

Bagge, V. (2011): Skik følge eller deal fly – få hjælp hos ambassader og konsulater, available at: http://www.youtube.com/watch?v=7sWR_1sLC3M&feature=youtu.be , 30st November, 2012.

Bargfeldt, E. (2012): Religion i Kina, available at: http://www.religion.dk/artikel/465691:Globalt-nyt--Religion-i-Kina--Religionsfrihed-under-kontrol, accessed 19th November, 2012.

Bertelsen, T.N. (2012): Korruption i Kina, available at: http://dk.gbtimes.com/nyheder/korruption-i-kina-er-massiv, accessed 27th November, 2012.

Björkman, I. & Kock, S. (1995), "Social relationships and business networks: the case of Western companies in China", *International Business Review*, Vol. 4, No. 4, pp. 519-535

Bryman, A. & Bell, E. (2011): *Business Research Methods*, 3rd Edition, Oxford University Press, Oxford.

Buus, I. (2004), "Leadership Development: A Scandinavian Model", *Business Leadership Review*, Vol. 1, No. 3.

Carroll, A.B. (1991), "The Pyramid of Corporate Social Responsibility" *Business Horizons,* Vol. 34, No. 4, pp. 39-48.

Carroll, A.B. (1999), "Corporate Social Responsibility – Evolution of a definitional construct", *Business & Society,* Vol. 38, No. 3, pp. 268-295.

Casey & Koleski (2011): U.S.-CHINA ECONOMIC AND SECURITY REVIEW COMMISSION REPPORT, http://www.uscc.gov/researchpapers/2011/12th-FiveYearPlan_062811.pdf, accessed 20th December, 2012,

Changingminds (2012): Halls Cultural Factors, available at: http://changingminds.org/explanations/culture/hall_culture.htm, accessed 22nd November, 2012.

Chen, M.J. (2001), *Inside Chinese Business: A Guide for Managers Worldwide,* Harvard Business School Press, Boston, MA.

Christiansen, T. (2011): Skik følge eller deal fly – få hjælp hos ambassader og konsulater, available at: http://www.youtube.com/watch?v=7sWR_1sLC3M&feature=youtu.be , accessed 30th November, 2012.

CSR Kompasset (2012a): Om ansvarlig leverandørstyring, available at: http://www.csrkompasset.dk/om-ansvarlig-leverand%C3%B8rstyring, 23rd November, 2012.

Dalgaard, B. (2012), "Kina vil være blød", *Ny Viden,* No. 10, pp. 14-16

Danish Innovation Center (2012): available at: http://icdk.um.dk/en/~/media/icdk/Documents/Shanghai/Key%20findings%20on%20Chinese%20innovation.pdf, accessed 20th December, 2012.

Danish Commerce and Companies Agency (2012): People and profit – a practical guide to corporate social responsibility, available at: http://www.eogs.dk/graphics/publikationer/CSR/Final%20OmO%20in%20WB%20edition-ny.pdf, accessed 23rd November, 2012.

de Wit, B. & Meyer, R. (2010): *Strategy: Process, Content, Context – An International Perspective,* 4th Edition, South- Western Cengage Learning, Hampshire.

Djursø, H.T. & Neergaard, P. (2006): *Social ansvarlighed – fra idealisme til forretningsprincipper,* Academica, Aarhus

Dvorak, R., Kaza, S. & Santhanam, N. (2012), "Three snapshots of Chinese innovation", *McKinsey Quarterly*, February, pp. 1-12.

European Commission (2011): A renewed EU strategy 2011-2014 for Corporate Social Responsibility, available at: http://eur-lex.europa.eu/LexUriServ/LexUriServ.do?uri=COM:2011:0681:FIN:EN:PDF, accessed 14th December, 2012

Fang, T. & Fletcher, R. (2006): Assessing the impact of culture on relationship creation and network formation in emerging Asian markets, available at: http://www.deepdyve.com/lp/emerald-publishing/assessing-the-impact-of-culture-on-relationship-creation-and-network-44AFi2OnGT, accessed 23rd November, 2012.

Fang, T. (2003), "A critique of Hofstede's fifth National Culture Dimension", *International Cultural Management*, Vol. 3, No. 3, pp. 347-368.

Fang, T. (2006): Negotiation: The Chinese Style, available at: www.emeraldinsight.com/0885-8624.htm, accessed 19th November, 2012.

Fang, T. (1999), *Chinese Business Negotiating style*, Thousand Oaks, SAGE Publications, Inc., California.

Faure, G.O. (1998), "Negotiation: the Chinese concept", *Negotiation Journal*, Vol. 14 No. 2, pp. 137-148.

Freeman, R.E & Liedtka, J. (1991), "Corporate Social Responsibility: A Critical Approach", *Business Horizons*, Vol. 34, No. 4, pp. 92-98.

Friedman, M. (1970), "The Social Responsibility of Business is to Increase its Profits", *The New York Times Magazine*, 13th September.

Fung, Y.L. (1966), *A Short History of Chinese Philosophy*, The Free Press, New York, NY.

Gesteland, R. (2002), *Cross-Cultural Business Behaviour*, Copenhagen Business School Press, 3rd Ed., Copenhagen.

Gadiesh, O., Leung, P. & Vestring, T. (2007), "The Battle for China's good-enough market", *Harvard Business Review*, Vol. 85, No. 9, pp. 81-89.

Graham, J.L. & Lam, N.M. (2004), "Doing Business in China", *Harvard Business Review* II series, pp. 31-56.

Gray, J.V., Roth, A.V. & Leiblein, M.J. (2011), "Quality risk in offshore manufacturing: Evidence from the pharmaceutical industry", *Journal of Operations Management*, Vol. 29, No. 7/8, pp. 737-752.

Handfield, R.B. (1994), "US Global Sourcing: Patterns of Development", *International Journal of Operations & Production Management*, Vol. 14, No. 6, pp. 40-51.

Hansen, C. R. (2012a): Kulturforståelse kræver selvindsigt, available at: http://www.cbs.dk/Micro/Insights-newsletter/Insights/Insights-CBS-2012/Nr.-3-2012/Kulturforstaaelse-kraever-selvindsigt, accessed 7th December, 2012.

Hansen, B. (2012b.): Derfor fejler Lars Larsen & B&O i Kina, available at: http://finans.tv2.dk/nyheder/article.php/id-49913815:derfor-fejler-lars-larsen-og-bo-i-kina.html, accessed 7th December, 2012.

Hansen, L. M. & Birk, K. (2012): Kina - en trussel eller mulighedernes land, available at: http://www.dr.dk/Undervisning/Gymnasium/Kina/%C3%98konomi/0123095756.htm, accessed 7th December, 2012.

Hansen, A.M. J. & Eiberg, K. (2012): Walk the talk, available at: http://www.kommunikationsforening.dk/Menu/Fagligt+nyt/Kommunikatøren/2001/Nr.+3+-+2001/walk+the+talk, accessed 26th November, 2012.

Haug, A. (2011), *Methodology*, power point presentation, Fall 2011, University of Southern Denmark.

History (2012): Mao Zedong - A Great Person of His Time, available at: http://history.cultural-China.com/en/46History9449.html, accessed 26th November, 2012.

Heizer, J. & Render, B. (2011): *Operations Management*, 10th Ed., Pearson Education Limited, Harlow.

Heldbjerg, G. & Haug, A. (2011): *Kompendium i Videnskabelige Undersøgelsesprocesser*, Syddansk Universitet, Kolding.

Hofstede, G. (2012a). *National Culture, Countries, What about China*, available at: http://geert-hofstede.com/China.html, accessed 23rd November, 2012.

Hofstede, G. (2012b), *National Culture, Countries, What about Denmark*, available at: http://geert-hofstede.com/denmark.html, accessed 24th November, 2012.

Hofstede, G. (1991), *Cultures and Organizations: Software of the Mind*, McGraw-Hill, New York.

Hofstede, G. & Bond, M.H. (1988), "The Confucius connection: from cultural roots to economic growth", *Organizational Dynamics*, Vol. 16 No. 4, pp. 4-21.

Holweg, M., Reichhart, A. & Hong, E. (2011), "On risk and cost in global sourcing", *International Journal of Production Economics*, Vol. 131, No. 1, pp. 333-341.

Institut for Menneskerettigheder (2007): CSR kompasset – landeprofil, Kina, available at: http://di.dk/SiteCollectionDocuments/Marked/CSR/Kina.pdf, accessed 25th May, 2012.

Kinkel, S. (2012), "Trends in production relocation and backshoring activities: Changing patterns in the course of global economic crisis", *International Journal of Operations & Production Management*, Vol. 32, No. 6, pp. 696-720.

Kruse, M. (2012): Megatrends Globale eller regionale, available at: http://www.cifs.dk/scripts/artikel.asp?id=1320&lng=1, accessed 30 November, 2012.

Lau, K.H. & Zhang, J. (2006), "Drivers and obstacles for outsourcing practices in China", *International Journal of Physical Distribution & Logistics Management*, Vol. 36, No. 10, pp. 776-79.

Leksikon (2012), Maoisme, available at: http://www.leksikon.org/art.php?n=1661, accessed 10th December, 2012.

Lim, J. (2012): Why China won't be innovative for at least 20 more years, *TechNode.com*, 26th March, 2012.

Luo, Y. (1997), "*Guanxi*: principles, philosophies, and implications", *Human Systems Management*, Vol. 16, No. 1, pp. 43-51.

Nie, W. (2010): China's one-child policy - success or failure, available at: http://www.bbc.co.uk/news/world-asia-pacific-11404623, accessed 29th November, 2012.

Nielsen, M., Sørensen, A. & Mauritzen, J. (2005): Culture report on China, available at: http://www.grin.com/en/e-book/109924/culture-report-on-China, accessed 20th November, 2012.

Nymark, J. (2012): Dyrt og svært eventyr, available at: http://borsen.dk.proxy3-bib.sdu.dk:2048/nyheder/avisen/artikel/11/25581/artikel.html?hl=b2c7c3bmcnQ7T2c7RHlydCBvZyBzduZydCBldmVudHlyO2R5cnQgb2c7ZXZlbnR5cjtkeXJ0O2R5cnQgZXZlbnR5cjtEeXJ0, accessed 27th November, 2012.

Murdoch, H. & Gould, D. (2004), *Corporate Social Responsibility in China: Mapping the Environment – A study commissioned by the global alliance for workers and communities*, GA publication series, Baltimore.

OECD (2012), Guidelines for multinational enterprise, available at: http://www.oecd.org/daf/internationalinvestment/guidelinesformultinationalenterprises/, accessed 6th December 2012.

Orr, G. & Roth, E. (2012), "A CEO's guide to innovation in China", *McKinsey Quarterly*, February, pp. 74-83.

Parisi, C., Mikkelsen, O.S., & Arlbjørn, J.S. (2009), "Implementing Corporate Social Responsibility in Supply Chains: Drivers and Barriers", In: Hertz, S. (ed.): *Proceedings of the 21st Annual NOFOMA Conference*, Jönköping International Business School, Jönköping, Sweden, pp. 648-663.

Peng, A.C. & Tjosvold, D. (2011), "Social face concerns and conflict avoidance of Chinese employees with their Western or Chinese managers", *Human Relations*, Vol. 64, No. 8, pp. 1031-1050.

Porkert, M. (1974): The Theoretical Foundations of Chinese Medicine: Systems of Correspondence, MIT press, Cambridge, Mass.

Prieto-Carrón, M., Lund-Thomsen, P., Chan, A., Muro, A. & Bhushan, C. (2006), "Critical Perspectives on CSR and Development: What We Know, What We Don't Know, and What We Need to Know", *International Affairs (Royal Institute of International Affairs 1994-)*, Vol. 82, No. 5, pp. 977-987.

Pub (2012): Kulturelle dimensioner, available at: http://pub.uvm.dk/2002/multikulturelvejledning/03.htm, accessed 24th November, 2012.

Porter, M. (1985): *Competitive advantage: Creating and sustaining superior performance*, Free Press, New York.

Religion (2012), Buddhisme, available at: http://www.religion.dk/buddhisme, accessed 19th February, 2013.

SAI (2012): SA 8000 Standard, available at: http://www.sa-ntl.org/index.cfm?fuseaction=Page.ViewPage&pageId=937, accessed 19th December, 2012.

Samfundsansvar (2012a): Principper og standarder, available at: www.samfundsansvar.dk/sw60620.asp, accessed 5th December, 2012.

Samfundsansvar (2012b), ISO 26000, available at: http://www.samfundsansvar.dk/sw61475.asp, accessed 5th December, 2012.

Schwartz, M. S. & Carroll, A. B. (2003), "Corporate Social Responsibility: A Three Domain Model" *Business Ethics Quarterly*. Vol. 13, No. 4, pp. 503–530.

Skov, M. (2007): Vi risikerer at gøre meget mere skade end gavn, available at: http://www.information.dk/146442.

Strand, R. (2010), "Culture & CSR: Embracing the Scandinavian Approach to CSR", in *Børsens Ledelsehåndbøger: Corporate Social Responsibility*, April, pp. 1-14, Børsens Forum, Copenhagen.

Silverstein, M., Liao, C., Singhi, A. & Michael, D. (2012): *The $10 trillion prize: Captivating the Newly Affluent in China and India*, Harvard Business Review Press, Boston.

Stanley, T. & Xu, V. (2011): KPMG China,- China´s 12th Five-Year Plan: Overview, March 2011, available at: http://www.kpmg.com/cn/en/IssuesAndInsights/ArticlesPublications/Documents/China-12th-Five-Year-Plan-Overview-201104.pdf, accessed 20th December, 2012.

Studwell, J. (2002): *The China Dream: The Elusive Quest for the Last Great Untapped Market on Earth*, Profile Books Ltd, London

Tidd, J. & Bessant, J. (2009): *Managing innovation - Integrating Technological Market and Organizational Change,* John Wiley & Sons ltd., Chichester.

Tidd, J. & Bessant, J. (2010): *Managing Innovation- Integrating Technological Market and Organizational Change,* 4th Ed., John Wiley & Sons, Ltd., Chichester.

Tidd, J. & Bessant, J. (2011): *Managing innovation*, John Wiley & Sons Ltd., West Sussex, England.

The Economist (2012): Enden er nær for Kina som billigt produktionsland, available at: http://www.business.dk/global/enden-er-naer-for-kina-som-billigt-produktionsland, accessed 29th November, 2012.

Trace, D., & Pisano, G. (1998), *Technology, organization, and competitiveness,* Oxford university press, New York.

Transparency International (2012): Corruption Perceptions Index 2012, available at: http://cpi.transparency.org/cpi2012/results/, accessed 5th December, 2012.

Tse, E., Jullens, J. & Russo, B. (2012), "China's Mid-Market Innovators", *Strategy+Business*, summer, pp. 1-6.

Tu, W.M. (1984): *Confucian Ethics Today: The Singapore Challenge*, Federal Publications, Singapore.

Udenrigsministeriet (2012): Landefakta Kina, available at: http://kina.um.dk/da/om-kina/landefakta-kina/, accessed 19th November, 2012.

UN Global Compact (2012): FN's Global Compact – Virksomheders Samfundsansvar, available at: www.unglobalcompact.org/languages/danish/index.html,accessed, 7th December, 2012.

Van Liempd, D. (2007): *An Introduction to Corporate Social Responsibility,* University of southern Denmark, Department of Entrepreneurship & Relationship Management, working paper series, 2007/3.

Van Marrewijk, M. (2003), "Concepts and Definitions of CSR and Corporate Social Sustainability: Between Agency and Communion", *Journal of Business Ethics*, Vol. 44, No. 2/3, pp. 96-97.

Wang, L. & H. (2009), "The Impact of Chinese Culture on Corporate Social Responsibility: The Harmony Approach", *Journal Business Ethics,* Vol. 88, No. 3, pp. 433-451.

Williamson, P.J. (2010), "Cost Innovation: Preparing for a "Value-for-Money" Revolution", *Long Range Planning,* Vol. 43, No. 2/3, pp. 343-353.

Winther, J. (2012): Korruption hæmmer danskere i Kina, available at: http://www.business.dk/industri/korruption-haemmer-danskere-i-kina, Accessed 16th December, 2012.

Wydra, N. (1996): *Feng Shui, The Book of Cures*, Contemporary Books, Chicago

Zeng, M. & Williamson, P.J. (2007): *Dragons at your door: How Chinese Cost Innovation Is Disrupting Global Competition*, Harvard Business School Publishing, Boston.

Xiaoping, X. (2012): venturebeat (Online), available at: http://venturebeat.com/2012/03/26/why-china-doesnt-innovate, accessed 20th December, 2012.

Yeung, I.Y.M. & Tung, R.L. (1996), "Achieving business success in Confucian societies: the importance of guanxi (connections)", *Organizational Dynamics*, Vol. 25, No. 2, pp. 54-65.

Yongqiang, G. (2009), "Corporate Social Performance in China: Evidence from Large Companies", *Journal of Business Ethics,* Vol. 89, No. 1, pp. 23-35.

Index

Alfa Laval; 16
Altercasting; 42
Beijing International Studies University; 16
Beijing International Studies University (BISU); 86
Brazilian culture; 147
Bredana Data System; 17
Bribery; 50
BRIC; 100
Buddhism; 37
Business cards; 27
Coloplast; 16
Communication barrier; 67
Confucianism; 26; 37
Copycats; 78
Corporate Social Responsibility; 115
Corruption; 50; 74
Cost innovation; 91
CSR pyramid; 119
Cultural learning; 148
Danfoss; 16
Danish consulate in Shanghai; 50
Danish embassy in Beijing; 50
Danish Innovation Center; 86
Deliberateness; 62
Department of Entrepreneurship and Relationship Management; 13
DISA; 16
Dynamic capabilities; 95
Emergentness; 62
Exploitation; 96
Exploration; 96
Face; 44; 77
Facilitating money; 74
Five year plan; 20
FLSmidth; 16
Good-enough market; 89
Group identification; 42
Guanxi; 26; 43; 79
Guoqing; 42
Hidden costs; 65; 72
Howe A/S; 17
Impressive experiences; 144
Individualism; 34
Infrastructure; 73
Innovation; 87; 96
Invention; 96
IPR; 78
ISO 26000; 130
Liangshou zhunbei; 44
Long term orientation; 36
Low market; 60
Mads Clausens Fond; 16
Masculinity/Femininity; 35
Mianxi; 26
Mid market; 60
Money Talks; 41
Monochronic; 36
National People's Congress; 23
Next 11; 100
Nilfisk; 15
Novo Nordisk; 16
Ole Kirks Fond; 16
One child policy; 76
Outsourcing; 61
People's Congresses; 23
Polychronic; 36
Power distance; 33
Premium market; 60
Renji Hexie; 44
SA 8000; 129
Scandinavian leadership style; 60
Shehui dengji; 44
Speed money; 74
Strategic formation; 61
Strategic Incrementalism; 63
Strategic Planning; 62

Tacit knowledge; 66; 68
Tame problem; 62
Taoism; 37
The business economy staff-student committee, University of Southern Denmark, Kolding; 16
The OECD Guidelines for Multinational Enterprises; 129
The People's Republic of China; 19
The Royal Danish Consulate General at Shanghai International Trade Center; 15
The Three Domain Model of CSR; 120
Toosbuys Fond; 17
Tresu Production Systems A/S; 17
Trust; 77
UN Global Compact.; 128
Uncertainty avoidance; 35
University of Southern Denmark; 13
Value-for-money revolution; 93
Viking Safe-Life Equipment; 17
Wicked problem; 62

About the Editors

Jan Stentoft Arlbjørn, Ph.D., is a Professor in Supply Chain Management (SCM) at the Department of Entrepreneurship and Relationship Management, University of Southern Denmark, Kolding. His research and teaching areas are within Supply Chain Management, Supply Chain Innovation, Enterprise Resource Planning, and Corporate Social Responsibility. He has practical industry experience from positions as Director (Program Management Office) at LEGO Systems A/S, Axapta, ERP Project Manager at Gumlink A/S, and as management consultant in a wide number of industrial enterprises from his own consulting practice.

Ole Stegmann Mikkelsen, Ph.D., is a Postdoc in Supply Chain Management (SCM) at the Department of Entrepreneurship and Relationship Management, University of Southern Denmark, Kolding. His research and teaching areas are within Supply Chain Management, Global Sourcing, Strategic Sourcing and Corporate Social Responsibility. He has published both nationally and internationally and has practical industrial experience from positions as Purchaser/Planner from Milliken Denmark A/S, and Strategic Purchasing Consultant and Director (Group Procurement Development and Support/finance) at Danfoss A/S.

Previous Field Study Projects

Arlbjørn, J.S. & de Haas, H. (Eds.) (2011) *Supply Chain Management: Brazil as an Emergent Economy*, University Press Southern Denmark, Odense.

Arlbjørn, J.S, de Haas, H. Ingstrup, M.B. & van Liempd, D. (Eds.) (2010) *Supply Chain Management: Business Operations in India*, University Press Southern Denmark, Odense.

Arlbjørn, J.S. & de Haas, H. (Eds.) (2009) *Supply Chain Management: Issues to Consider when doing business in China*, Academica, Aarhus.